THE FULCRUM-CENTRIC PLAN
for Emerging and High Potential Leaders

LEADERSHIP
IN
BALANCE

Mike Lerario

LIEUTENANT COLONEL (U.S. Army, Retired)

Published by
Hasmark Publishing
judy@hasmarkpublishing.com

Editor:
Sigrid Macdonald

Cover Design and Interior Layout:
Anne Karklins
annekarklins@gmail.com

ISBN-13: 978-1-988071-19-0
ISBN-10: 1-988071-19-4

This book is dedicated to my loving wife, Martha;
I couldn't have done this or much else in my life
without her by my side.

ACKNOWLEDGMENTS

I would like to acknowledge the invaluable assistance of Anney Smith, my coach, for helping me make this book a reality. It existed only in my thoughts for over ten years but with her assistance and support, it moved from the private recesses of my mind to the pages you are now reading. I started this journey with the idea that Anney would help me understand the intricacies of getting a book published but discovered that she could help me with so much more than that. I have found in her a coach and a friend for life.

My colleagues of The Wexford Group International; the smartest and most dedicated professionals I have ever had the honor to work with. I've learned so much from them and continue to count on them for council and advice. In particular, I'd like to acknowledge the men who have encouraged me to write this book: Hank Kinnison, Randy Sullivan, Pete Arsenault, Gene Zink, Kevin McEnery, Mike Stewart, Jack Silvers, Ron Russell, Jim Kaiser, CD, Scott Flanagan, Morgan Darwin, Pat McNamara and especially Gary Riccio and Bill McDonough who have been as excited about this project (if not more so) as I have been.

All the men and women that I have ever served with while I was on active duty. The "quiet professionals" of the Joint Special Operations Command, in particular two of my former bosses, Bill McRaven and Tony Thomas, stand out as examples of balanced leadership. I will forever be tied to the soldiers of 2-505 PIR, D/2-325 AIR, D/1-17 CAV (LRS) and especially 2nd Platoon B/3-325 where I first grew as a leader. Throughout my career, whenever I had the privilege to command soldiers, their impact on me was incalculable and I always got more than I gave. These are my band of brothers…

A special thanks to Chris Whitaker for his encouragement to write this book while we served together in Iraq; he has remained a steadfast friend and has forced me to think more deeply.

To Joe Stimac for all his sound advice and friendship and his inspiration to always ask the right questions.

Cecilia Clark for her example of hard work and determination in everything she does and for the insights she has provided on this and other projects.

To Rob Nielsen and my colleagues at All American Leadership; you've made me dig deeper into the most current thinking on leadership and you challenge me to be an elite member of an elite team.

Thanks to Judy O'Beirn and her team at Hasmark Publishing for their work to edit and prepare the manuscript for publication. And especially Sigrid Macdonald for her editing of the manuscript and Jenn Gibson for helping to keep me on task.

To Matt McCreary who helped me to develop the "Leadership Fulcrum Assessment" in a relationship that started as we worked together in Afghanistan but one that will last forever. Also, my colleagues at RAND, Matt Boyer and Matt Lewis, for their insights and advice on this and many other things. And to the team at GCorp for binging the LFA on-line in more ways than one.

Carlos Vasquez and his team at QuadexMedia for building the "be the fulcrum®" website.

Father (COL, Retired) Owen J. Mullen who has been my spiritual advisor and great friend throughout all the stages of my career.

To my good friends in Fayetteville and the Army for their support and encouragement across a lifetime of experiences, especially Melanie and Mark Erwin; Linda and Mac Healy; and Jennifer Sullivan, who gave up her "pied-a-terre" in Wrightsville Beach so I could do some serious writing.

I also owe a debt to my classmates, company mates and rugby teammates from USMA '83 – Proud to Be – especially our Mullet-toss friends…

My in-laws, Joan and COL (Ret) Hank Harrison were my first examples to a life in the Army and to a life after the Army. Their help and love have always been there and their contribution to this effort is incalculable.

To my family: my parents, Pete and Louise Lerario, who gave me the foundations of leadership with their love and support throughout my life; my brother Tom and sister Marisa who have kept me in line when I needed it and supported me unconditionally – their spouses do the same for us all now.

My sons, Dominic and Harrison: you are the best things I've ever helped to create and you have made me so proud by being the men you have become. The rest of the DELF crew, you bring more joy into my life than you could ever know.

And finally, to Martha: my wife, my best friend and my fulcrum for finding balance in my life. You have always been there for me and you have always believed in me. I love you with all my heart…

TABLE OF CONTENTS

INTRODUCTION

Give me a lever long enough and a fulcrum on which to place it and
I shall move the world.[1]
~ Archimedes

My Leadership Journey

For the better part of forty years, nearly all of my adult life, I have been on a journey of leadership. Always a student, usually a practitioner, I have developed as a leader with a mix of education and on-the-job training.

In the early days, what I learned and what I knew about leadership came mostly from role models; my father and my mother, my football and track coaches and later my instructors and peers at the United States Military Academy. I saw early on that you can learn as much from a poor example as you can from a great example and lucky for me, I had mostly great examples.

At West Point, the leadership lessons extended from the classroom through the barracks, on athletic fields and during our summer training. I was lucky to play rugby and have some of the best friends I would ever know and ever have on my team. They were also some of the greatest leaders I have seen. As I write this, three of them are three-star generals.

The officers I had contact with were also incredible examples. Most were also Academy graduates and many had seen combat in Vietnam. These men (they were almost exclusively males back in the late '70s and early

---

1. http://www.brainyquote.com/quotes/quotes/a/archimedes101761.html

'80s) knew and lived by the cardinal rules of leadership: lead by example; give all orders in your own name; the mission comes first but you must take care of your people; be clear in your communications.

I graduated from the Military Academy in May of 1983, a brand new infantry officer headed to Fort Benning Georgia for Infantry Officer Basic and Ranger School. Newly minted and sporting the coveted black and gold Ranger Tab, I joined my first unit at Fort Bragg, NC: 2nd Platoon, Bravo Company, 3rd Battalion, 325th Airborne Infantry of the 82nd Airborne Division.

B/3-325 is the military notation for that unit and at the time, it was part of an experiment for the Army called COHORT–Cohesion, Operational Readiness, Training–a program designed to build more cohesive units by keeping them together longer. At the platoon and company level, it was a great success but when expanded to battalion level, it was too big, unwieldy and unpopular so the Army killed the program. For me, it had a huge impact on my outlook on leadership and on life. We never had to serve in combat together but the men of that platoon are my brothers still today.

I stayed with paratroopers at Fort Bragg, in Vicenza, Italy and back to Fort Bragg for the next eight years. I led two platoons for a total of twenty-seven months and commanded two companies for a total of forty-three months, eight of those months in Saudi Arabia and Iraq for Operation Desert Shield/Desert Storm. All of those leadership opportunities came before my thirty-first birthday; truly one of the best things about an Army career is the opportunity to lead and have an impact on people's lives at a young age.

The rest of my Army career was full of development opportunities with schools and assignments. The apex of my career was commanding a 750-man parachute infantry battalion in the 82nd Airborne. We deployed to Afghanistan in 2003 and with attached units, our average size was 1200 men and women. My final assignment on active duty was with the Joint Special Operations Command and in that job, I found myself in and out of Afghanistan and Iraq for the remaining three years of my service.

These last two assignments allowed me to work for and with some of the greatest leaders in the modern military: John Campbell, Stan McChrystal, Bill McRaven and Tony Thomas to name a few. At forty-five years of age, I was still watching role models and learning a thing or two about leadership while serving as a leader too. For the twenty-seven years that I wore a uniform as a cadet and as an infantry officer, I got the chance to learn something about leadership and to practice something about leadership every day.

For the last ten years, since my retirement from active duty, I have worked as a consultant. I've worked with military and government organizations and I've worked with private industry and the thing that stands out the most to me is what great opportunity the Army gave me to study and practice leadership – an opportunity few outside the military can experience.

I have a Master's degree in leadership development that I earned in 1994 while assigned back to West Point as a tactical officer. A company tactical officer is the official and legal commander of a company (about 120) of cadets and my graduate program was known as the Eisenhower Fellowship in Leadership Development. That was the first time since my cadet days that I actually (had to) read books on leadership. They were required. Most were textbooks but I do remember reading the works of Stephen Covey and thinking there was some pretty good and useful stuff in there.

In the last ten years and with my work as a consultant, I've been reading leadership books again but this time because I want to. There is an amazing wealth of information, ideas and knowledge out there for the taking and most of it is pretty good. Books by the likes of Collins, Marquet, Goldsmith, Sinek, Dweck and Goleman are bestsellers for a reason and company I'd like to keep. But for all the knowledge that is out there, I feel that there is a perspective that is missing and it's a perspective that any leader can benefit from but especially new and emerging leaders.

All in all, I have nearly forty years of experience with leading, following and leadership as an academic exercise. Over the years, I have seen and been a part of some amazing leadership successes but also some major leadership failures. In all that time, one great question nagged me: how do some seemingly talented people do so well in some situations but fail so miserably in others? This question and my experiences have led me to a perspective of leadership which I will share with you here.

That perspective is what I call "Fulcrum-centric Leadership." It is my perspective and point of view of the four critical domains every leader must master. Unlike other perspectives which might argue that there is one best way to lead or a hierarchy of leadership practices, I'm here to tell you that any and all leader actions can be positive or negative depending on the situation and how you apply yourself to it.

Fulcrum-centric Leadership is about understanding your natural tendency in each of the four domains and then assessing the situation that you are leading and, when needed, shifting from your tendency in order to achieve balance.

This Book Is for You...

This book is written for the new manager or someone who aspires to become a leader. Whether you have just finished school or have been working for some time, you are in (or about to assume) your first real leadership position. What now?

As a manager/leader, you will have to manage resources and make decisions; you will have to prioritize and you will have to motivate. While culture and organizational structure all factor into this, leadership is very much an individual skill in a team sport–you are now a key player, like the quarterback on a football team. Therefore, this book and the recommendations I make begin with you. There will always be a time and a place to discuss the impact of culture, the nature of trust and the importance of emotional intelligence when talking about leaders and leadership but those topics are secondary to the topic of you and your leadership tendencies.

This book will help you to see and understand your natural tendency in each of four critical leadership domains. Once you've identified your true and natural tendency, you become self-aware of your default position as a leader. Armed with that knowledge, and as you become situationally aware of your team and the environment, you will learn to see when the situation demands a shift away from that tendency in order to find balance between you and the environment where you lead.

I'm not going to ask you to change your default position or tendency in these domains; that could lead you down the path of being a phony. But understanding how you naturally want to communicate or influence, how you assess and make decisions or where you focus will give you clarity to choose to be different when things aren't going well or when you need to accomplish more.

I'm not going to ask you to change your team, your boss, your customers, your competition or anything else in the environment. While that might be possible, it would take more time than you probably have to solve today's leadership problem. Effective leadership is about building long-term success but it begins with the situation that exists right now. Your first job is to be effective now.

So, where does that leave you? It leaves you, the leader, in a position to understand yourself, to understand the situation and to shift how you operate in each of the critical domains of leadership when the situation demands it.

This Book Is Also For...

Executives, supervisors and human resource professionals looking for new talent will also find this book useful. The leadership domains and their opposing tendencies provide you with an outline to find individuals with the ability to balance their leadership tendencies to any situation. Talent is good but talent is never enough. Understanding the concepts of *Leadership in Balance* will help you define what you need your junior leaders to be able to do now and in the future.

Fulcrum-centric Leadership Defined

It's my experience that simple concepts are not only easier for most people to understand, they often provide the best solutions. Certainly, there are complex issues and problems that require complex explanations but there is a lot out there that can be classified in some sort of binary state: on or off; yes or no; one or zero. That's not to say that the idea of finding a "both/and" solution is wrong. It's just to say that in many cases, certainly in the extreme, things can be classified as either one thing or its opposite.

As an example in nature, things are either in balance or out of balance; the first instance is marked by a calm and harmony and the second is marked by conflict and struggle–a struggle to regain balance.

Fulcrum-centric Leadership is my way to simplify the concepts of leadership yet at the same time making sure that it is a comprehensive description and an effective system. It's my belief that leadership is an activity and a discipline that can and should find balance in how it is understood and applied. But in this case, I am not talking about balance like a balance scale but balance like a "seesaw." Both have a lever and a pivot or fulcrum but the image is very different.

With a scale, we learn the measure of some unknown quantity by adding known amounts to the other side of the scale. When they are balanced, we now know the specific amount of the item being measured. But in the real world, balance is achieved against a constant shift of forces in the environment – do one thing and it shifts the balance making equilibrium difficult. If this were not the case, leadership would be easy and once the right measure was found for an individual or an organization, nothing would ever need to be changed.

Instead of a scale, I want you to see Fulcrum-centric Leadership as two kids on a playground trying to use a seesaw (or teeter-totter depending on where you grew up…). If the children are equal weight, they have balance and can easily "ride" the seesaw, going back and forth, up and down. If, however, one of the kids weighs more than the other, it becomes harder to ride because the seesaw will want to stay down on the side of the larger kid.

Now imagine the same two kids, one significantly larger than the other. If the imbalance in weight is significant, the big kid will stay on the ground and the little kid will be stuck up in the air. Not a lot of fun for anyone unless the bigger kid is also a bully and then he's having the time of his life. But if the heavier kid moves in towards the fulcrum on the seesaw, the weight differential is negated and the two kids can find balance and play together as they ride.

I know it's not politically correct to say but in the days of my youth, we might have called that much bigger kid the "fat kid." Your natural tendency for different traits or characteristics can be your "inner fat kid."

There, I said it. To keep from saying it again and making this book one big controversy about body image, I'll take a cue from my military background and create an acronym. From now on, we will refer to your tendency of being overweight in any characteristic as your IFK (your "inner fat kid"). It's possible that your tendency may be underweight for the situation as well, making it your ISK ("inner skinny kid").

So, if you let it, your IFK will be a bully and your ISK will be helpless and both will keep you and your situation out of balance. Therefore, the skill in leadership becomes knowing when and how to move the fulcrum to regain balance.

This book sets out to help both the student and the practitioner of leadership understand their natural tendency in four major leadership characteristics and provides instruction on how to achieve balance when that natural preference is out of balance with the current situation.

This concept of Fulcrum-centric Leadership depends on three things: understanding yourself, understanding the situation and acting to shift the balance when the situation demands it. The situation is a broad term covering everything that is external to you, the leader: senior leadership, subordinates, stakeholders, clients, weather, resources, tasks, etc. Balance comes in understanding one's natural tendency and desire and how to find balance with the forces in the situation that weigh against that natural position.

The chapters of this book will focus on four separate characteristics of leadership, defining each domain and its polar opposite tendencies. In general, the opposite tendencies can be characterized as either inclusive or exclusive depending on which extreme they fall. This gives us eight unique tendencies to describe one's natural leadership style.

Domain				
Tendency	Communications	Adaptability	Focus	Influence
Exclusive	Transmit	Rigid	Selfish	Control
Inclusive	Receive	Flexible	Selfless	Command

You might be tempted to assign a positive value to the inclusive tendencies and a negative value to the exclusive tendencies but that would be a gross generalization. Achieving balance might (and often does) require more weight in a particular tendency for any given situation; resisting something that at face-value seems negative is a huge mistake if and when it is the thing needed to achieve balance in that situation. These tendencies exist together in each domain; in fact, they couldn't exist without each other. If we didn't have selfish, there would be no selfless.

Of the four domains, focus will probably cause you the greatest pain to understand and to act. We have such a huge cultural bias against selfishness that even when we can be honest with ourselves about our focus or our motivation, we have a very hard time admitting that to anyone else. More often than not, we will fail to act in even the smallest way selfish because of this cultural bias and, in doing so, miss out on a great opportunity or withhold our gifts and talents from the world.

Now, I'm not suggesting that we all become more selfish, just that we become more self-aware of our tendency for focus and act in a way that is best suited to the situation.

Communications, adaptability and influence are easier to adjust our position on because they come with less baggage associated with the exclusive tendency. The key to success in your leadership journey is to not fall victim to your natural tendency but instead to be honest with yourself and know how and when to move off that tendency, even when that means taking on a more "negative" tendency.

Why This Understanding of Fulcrum-centric Leadership Is Important

First and foremost, Fulcrum-centric Leadership requires (and improves) self-awareness, which in itself is a good thing. Whether we call it mindfulness, attention control or presence, knowing yourself and your tendencies is a first step in being better at any and everything you do.

It is also important because real leadership demands balance as every situation and every individual is different; no matter how small or nuanced the difference, a leader must understand herself and her situation to lead effectively. I became an adult as I became a soldier and most of what I have learned about leadership (good and bad) came from my experiences as a soldier. I've worked for the "leader" who used intimidation and threats to influence his people. The organizations they were in charge of succeeded more in spite of them than because of them.

While it is true that most leaders have the power to hire and fire their subordinates, or at least to affect their future in some positive or negative way, authority that is backed only by a punitive code is not leadership. True leadership is about influence and vision, decision making and communication. In the authority only case, the best a "leader" can achieve within his/her team is compliance (with the exception of the sycophant who sees opportunity in riding the coattails of this tyrant) while in the true leadership case, what follows the leader is commitment and energy.

Balance isn't about equality or an equal measure of the opposing tendencies; balance is about equilibrium between your natural tendency and the environment. Your tendencies are fairly well established but they are not fixed. The environment is very much dynamic, constantly changing and adjusting to uncountable variables. This is why you are the solution to any imbalance in your life, in your work and with your team. Learn to "be" the fulcrum and you can accomplish anything.

While I will not dwell much on your relationship with your boss in this book, it is an important aspect of leadership in the "real world." So, what happens when you find yourself in charge of a group but your boss is a terrible leader and by terrible I mean anything from just simple incompetence to outright evil? How do you find balance in an organization that allows for that kind of "leadership" so long as your boss doesn't do (or isn't caught doing) something illegal or immoral? Your job is to find balance with that boss; to lead your people the best way you can but to manage the negative tendencies in your boss. You can't change him, you shouldn't change yourself, but you have to be the fulcrum in the relationship. Move the fulcrum and you restore balance to the situation. If you can't restore balance, you could find employment someplace else, but that's a subject for another book…

This book will help you understand yourself, understand your environment and understand how to regain or achieve balance by moving the fulcrum.

- Understand Self
- Understand the Environment
- Move (be) the Fulcrum

Are Great Leaders Born or Made?

I love this question. It ranks up there with "Which came first, the chicken or the egg?"

Of course, leaders are born. We are all born; born with different traits, characteristics and abilities. But not everyone uses their talents to the best effect. An athlete with slightly above average skill can compensate with hard work and determination to become a great player. Some call this Grit (the Cleveland Indians have even turned it into an acronym: Growth mindset, Routine, Individual mechanics, Team first approach) but there is no doubt that we can all become better, even elite, if we put in the work. Therefore, great leaders are born AND made.

An example of this is the playground (again). You can watch little children playing together and there are always one or two kids who stand out – they organize (or dominate) the rest of the kids; they become the captains and pick teams. They didn't have any formal training in leadership; it just comes naturally to them when they decide to organize the rest of the playground. But what happens to those kids once they grow up? The ones doing the picking don't always go on to do great things in life and the ones picked last sometimes become great leaders (if I had to guess, Steve Jobs was probably picked last most of the time when teams were picked on the playground).

So, leaders are born and they are made and how good they are is often a function of how they use what they were born with and how they learn to improve and grow in every area possible. And that is why I keep going back to the playground. For most of us, our first leadership experience is in playing games or sports and our first experience in play with others (and this is important because leadership is a social science) is on the playground. The image of the two children on the playground seesaw, one much heavier than the other, combines all these issues: our initial experiences in leadership and our desire and need to achieve balance.

While I hope that any and all leaders can learn and grow from this view of leadership and finding balance, it is the junior or emerging leader I will focus on. More senior leaders are probably too wedded to their tendencies or have already figured this out to some degree. For senior executives, this book can be instructive in what to look for in the new employees and managers that you hire.

What Does It Mean to "Be the Fulcrum?"

In simple mechanics, a seesaw is a class one lever. Effort is exerted on one side to move a load with the help of a fulcrum.

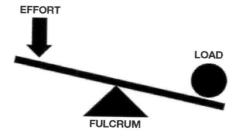

In this model, you (the leader) are the effort. The situation (everything in the environment that is external to you) is the load. For most of our discussion in *Leadership in Balance*, we will concern ourselves with the team you are leading when talking about the situation. The lever in this model is one of the four leadership domains and the fulcrum is the point that supports the lever and where the lever pivots.

Where you currently sit on the lever of each domain is your natural tendency. If your tendency is way out on one end or the other of the lever, it's an IFK; if you allow it to dominate in that domain, you'll be left sitting on the ground; you'll leave everyone on your team or in the environment up in the air. Before too long, if left unchecked, no one will want to get on the seesaw with you.

If your tendency is close to the center of the domain lever, it doesn't mean that you will naturally find balance; in fact, the slightest change in the situation could cause a huge imbalance when your natural tendency is close to the center of the lever. It might also mean that you have a harder time moving towards one of the extreme ends of the domain when and if the situation dictates you to lead in that way.

You must learn and understand your natural tendency in each of the four leadership domains and, when they are out of balance with the situation, apply more effort in the tendency appropriate to gain balance with the situation.

Going back to the example where your tendency is close to the extreme end of the lever, because you can't actually move the fulcrum on a seesaw, finding balance comes from shortening the lever on the effort side or, in other words, moving away from your natural tendency and towards the opposite characteristic tendency, closer to the fulcrum. If you find that communications are out of balance and you are a natural "transmit" leader, you must learn to move closer to "receive" in order to restore balance.

At this point, you might ask: "But what if I'm close to the center already?" or "What if my natural tendency isn't way out on the end of the lever?"

These are great questions and here is your answer.

First, the Fulcrum-centric Leadership model isn't about finding balance between the two tendencies of these four domains; it's about balancing your tendency in that domain with whatever is going on in that situation. Remember, you are the "effort" and the situation is the "load."

Second, as mentioned, your tendency doesn't have to be an IFK; it might be an ISK ("inner skinny kid" – also not PC). In that case, it's possible that in a given situation when you become the fulcrum, you aren't moving towards your opposite tendency but more to the extreme of your natural tendency. So, the issue with Leadership in Balance is knowing how and when to be the fulcrum and how far and in which direction to move.

Leadership Fulcrum Assessment

The Leadership Fulcrum Assessment (LFA) is the instrument I've developed to help you understand your natural tendency. Scores for each domain range from 10 at the far exclusive end of the lever and 50 at the far inclusive end of the lever. If you score close to a 10 or a 50, your natural tendency has great potential to be an IFK. If you score close to a 30, your natural tendency has great potential to be an ISK.

The Leadership Fulcrum Assessment is behaviorally based, meaning it asks you to score yourself based on how you have behaved in the past, not what you think about the tendency or what you might do hypothetically. From my work in assessing and selecting high performing candidates, I learned from Joe Stimac of AccuHire that past performance is the best indicator of future performance. That same tenet applies here in understanding your tendency.

Your natural tendency and your score on the Leadership Fulcrum Assessment are more about the frequency or quantity of your tendencies as a leader. Once you learn to "be the fulcrum," you will see that finding balance is about quality and quantity of your actions in that domain.

The chapters of this book will provide you with strategies and drills to become the fulcrum, restoring balance to that domain of leadership when you and the situation are imbalanced. While the four domains can influence each other to some extent, we will look at each in isolation for purposes of clarity and simplicity. This allows the chapters of the book to stand alone and be read in any sequence depending on what domain you want to work on.

Before we dive into the specifics of each domain, I want to explain them and the idea of exclusive and inclusive tendencies in the next chapter. Then we'll look at communications, adaptability, focus and influence separately. To take the LFA, go now to: www.bethefulcrum.com and use promotion code CRISPIAN1415 when you sign up to take the assessment and there will be no charge as my gift to you for purchasing this book.

DOMAINS AND THEIR TENDENCIES:
COMMUNICATIONS
ADAPTABILITY
FOCUS
INFLUENCE

At this point, you might ask: "What about emotional intelligence?" "What about mindset?" "What about mindfulness?" "What about (insert favorite leadership/leader paradigm here…)?"

First, I don't discount the importance and value of any of the things listed above. Emotional intelligence is hugely important but it is a product of self-awareness and understanding the environment around you. There are elements of emotional intelligence that are embedded in the domains of communications and focus. The same goes for mindfulness, which can be described as meditation or presence. It is still about self-awareness at its most basic level. Again, it is my belief that leadership is the function of many factors but the four main domains, and the four that I will address in these pages, are Communications, Adaptability, Focus and Influence. Through self-awareness, situational awareness and knowing how, when and where to move the fulcrum, all of us can be great leaders and the teams we lead will be great too.

Fulcrum-centric Leadership does not replace any of these other concepts; it merely simplifies and consolidates them into the four critical domains. While this chart is by no means complete, it is a start at aligning other leadership concepts with the Fulcrum-centric Leadership domains.

Domain	Communications	Adaptability	Focus	Influence
Other Paradigms	Emotional Intelligence (EQ); Learning Styles; Body Language	Mindset; GRIT; Decision Making	Servant Leader; EQ; Trust	Leader-Leader; Purpose; Trust

In defining these central domains and their tendencies, it is important to look at them in the extreme. Let me say that again: it's important to look at them in the extreme; the 100% condition of that tendency. The extreme case is found at the opposite ends of the lever – the ends of the seesaw. In a perfect world, the neutral point – equally exclusive and inclusive – would always rest above the fulcrum in the exact center of the lever. But the world and the people who inhabit it are never perfect. In the real world, we have tendencies and biases and we occupy someplace on the lever between the two extremes.

Tendencies

Each of the four domains that we will examine in this book has two opposite conditions or characteristics that we will call tendencies. They exist with and because of each other; you cannot have just one by itself.

It has been my experience that all things that involve humans and human nature exist in one or the other of these characteristics. They are the exclusive at one end and the inclusive at the other end.

The exclusive is all about the entity (individual, team or organization) that we are observing; everything else comes second. In general, the tendencies that occupy the exclusive end of the domain carry a negative connotation. These tendencies resist and even exclude participation and influence from the environment.

By contrast, the inclusive tendencies are open to inputs and influences from the environment. They carry a generally positive connotation and if you asked people which tendencies were good and which were bad, most would certainly be in the inclusive camp.

Using the seesaw image and analogy for finding balance, the four domains and their tendencies might look like this. I've kept the exclusive tendencies on the left side of the seesaw and the inclusive tendencies on the right side:

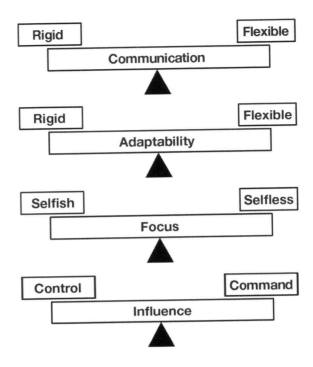

Exclusive

In the extreme, exclusive tendencies box out all other participants, information and facts in the execution of leadership duties and tasks. While this can lead to quick decisive action when the leader is experienced and is working in familiar areas, it can cause the leader or his/her organization to be ostracized by peers or rendered ineffective when everyone is afraid to act because the boss holds all the authority. You may have already worked with or for someone who only talks and never listens; always holds on to an idea or decision, never changing or adjusting to conditions that change; always puts their interest first, never the interests of others; and always micro-manages and never empowers others to accomplish tasks.

Inclusive

In the extreme, inclusive tendencies bring all other participants and information into the execution of leadership duties and tasks. While this can lead to greater ownership by everyone associated with the tasks or missions at hand, it can be slow and indecisive when the leader waits for all stakeholders to provide input or to acquiesce. Just the opposite of someone who leads with strong exclusive tendencies, you might have seen the leader who always listens but never articulates a plan or idea; always changes their mind and can never commit to a course of action; always thinks of others and never puts themselves first; and always leads by providing a vision but never gives guidance.

Communications is central to every relationship but most certainly in the relationship between leaders and their teams. We might call the members of these teams followers but, in their own right, they are also leaders in how they execute their tasks and how they interact with other members of the team and the boss. This idea of the follower as leader is nicely described by L. David Marquet in his book Turn the Ship Around. It is a compelling story with communications being a central part of how the leader (Marquet) was able to get his boat (submarines are boats, not ships) and his crew to become one of the finest in the U.S. Navy.

The extreme tendencies of communications are transmit and receive. You have a tendency to either send out information, directions, advice, policy, etc. or you have a tendency to take in the same. We think of the first as "talkers" and the second as "listeners." While the acts of transmission and reception are seemingly active and passive respectively, this is not necessarily the case. You can just as easily speak without giving it much thought and you can very actively listen. That said, for our purposes, transmit is the exclusive domain because, in the extreme, it is all about the sender and what message they want to send. Receive is the inclusive tendency because in the extreme, it is all about taking in the message from someone (or someplace) else. When you transmit, you allow others access to your thoughts; when you receive, you allow others to influence your thought process. This distinction is why I place transmitting in the exclusive domain and receiving in the inclusive domain.

Adaptability is an important leadership domain because leaders must be both proactive and responsive to the task at hand and to the situation. But here is the important part: the situation is never static. The situation is always dynamic and what worked yesterday or even what works today may not work tomorrow or at some point in the future. The solution that works excellently in the short-term may be exactly the worst thing in the long-term. While adaptability involves initiative and decision making, it is just as important in defining what happens after the decision has been made and the plan has been set into motion.

The opposing tendencies of adaptability are rigid and flexible. When we stick to what we "know" is right, we are rigid in our thoughts, even if we are correct, because the situation never stays unchanged by our actions and our decisions. When we are open to the entire realm of the possible, we are flexible in making and sticking with decisions. Rigid is the exclusive tendency because in the extreme, a rigid leader cannot get outside of his world or world view. Flexible, in contrast, is the inclusive tendency because, in the extreme, the flexible leader will change his mind or decisions as new information and facts are presented – in the extreme that can cause uncertainty and ambiguity as the team has to constantly react to a leader always changing their mind.

Focus is the domain that defines who or what we are working for. Team and the greater good are essential aspects of leadership because if we only had to lead ourselves, we would simply call it discipline. Leadership is the art and science of getting individuals to perform at their best, independently and collectively as a team, so focus is not about outcomes but motivation to achieve those outcomes. We can be motivated for our own self or we can be motivated for something bigger than ourselves.

The opposing tendencies of focus are selfish and selfless. When the leader is motivated by recognition and advancement of self, he is said to be selfish. When the leader is motivated by a greater good, the team or some noble cause, we call that leader selfless. In the extreme, selfish is detrimental to a broader community and can potentially be bad for the leader given the societal bias against selfishness. That said, a drive for some personal idea or desire is often the catalyst for great invention or change that is beneficial to society at large. Selflessness in the extreme is foregoing any and all personal benefit for the good of others – even to the point of sacrificing one's very life. While selflessness is held almost universally as a virtue, it can be a crutch that leaders lean on, allowing them not to take that bold step to advance a personal idea or to take on greater responsibility or authority.

Influence is the final domain of the Fulcrum-centric Leadership perspective but it is the essential task of leadership and therefore, in my mind, the first among equals. Whether it's a mundane or dangerous task, the leader must get the team to accomplish it. While doing the minimum is good enough by definition, we value excellence; great leaders and great teams are happy with nothing less. In the case of the mundane task, the leader's influence must motivate subordinates to overcome complacency and inattention to detail; in the case of the dangerous task, the leader must motivate subordinates to overcome fear and see the value in the outcome no matter the sacrifice it may entail.

The tendencies of influence are control and command. Control is needed most when the team is immature or inexperienced to the task or the environment. While it can often show up as "micro-management," it is sometimes the only management that will work. Command is the ability to indirectly achieve an outcome and it is most associated with intent and purpose. The leader who commands well ensures that his subordinates are ready, willing and able to accomplish the task with the minimum amount of guidance and direction. While this is almost universally seen as the epitome of leadership, if the subordinates are not mature enough or experienced enough to deal with a command style of leadership, they and the organization will have difficulty at best and will, in the worst case, experience abject failure.

While there is a certain amount of impact that the four domains have on each other – for example, communications and influence are nearly inseparable – the intent of this book is to look at each domain more or less in isolation. In learning each by itself, you will be better able to understand your natural tendency in that domain and learn how to be the fulcrum when the situation demands it of you.

You are ready now to gain a clear understanding of your tendency in each of the four domains. If you haven't done so already, take the Leadership Fulcrum Assessment at www.bethefulcrum.com and remember to use the code CRISPIAN1415. Go now so you have awareness of your natural tendency of leading in each domain before we go into the details on each.

COMMUNICATIONS

Communications

Communication: *noun* com·mu·ni·ca·tion \kŏ-myü-nĭ-'kā-shŭn\

> : the act or process of using words, sounds, signs, or behaviors to express or exchange information or to express your ideas, thoughts, feelings, etc., to someone else

> : a message that is given to someone : a letter, telephone call, etc.

communications

> : the ways of sending information to people by using technology[2]

Communications Defined

As we discussed earlier, the tendencies of communication are "transmit" at the exclusive end and "receive" at the inclusive end. On the face of it, this might seem backwards because when we are transmitting in communication, we are sending some message out to other people. While the mechanics of that are true, it's what's going on within us that determines the exclusive versus inclusive nature of communications.

---

2. http://www.merriam-webster.com/dictionary/communications

Experts acknowledge, and in survey after survey, effective communications rank as one of the most important elements in having a successful organization. I believe that communications is also a central aspect of leadership – you cannot be an effective leader if you cannot communicate effectively. Yet for effective communications, we have to both transmit and receive.[3]

The bottom line is this: you need the ability to receive the information and facts (good and bad) that will allow you as a leader to make sound decisions and choices. You also need the ability to transmit to your team (your boss and stakeholders too) the information and facts they need to make decisions and get their work done. Vision, purpose and goals are a part of this as well because you have to receive inputs to what these things are or ought to be and then you must articulate them back out to the team. This is why communications is the first of four domains we must assess and work on to be a better and more effective leader.

When we transmit, we are sending a signal or a message. The thought and energy that went into that message was either originated by the sender or originated by some other source (higher HQ, the boss, etc.) and relayed by the sender. In both cases, the sender has to think about the message and how they are communicating it and this is a purely internal process. It will stay that way unless and until the sender takes in feedback or is willing to listen to how the message was received and whether or not the content of that message is valid or accepted.

The most extreme example of transmit as an exclusive leadership tendency is the leader who does all the talking and when they should be listening, they are really thinking about what they will transmit next.

One of the most insightful things that I ever heard was the idea that communications is 100% receiver: it doesn't matter what I say, it's what you heard that matters. While this is a simple summary of the process, it highlights the fact that clarity and understanding in communications usually lies not with the sender but with the receiver. Balance in communications happens when we understand our obligation to transmit clearly and to receive openly.

---

3. "Why Communication Is Today's Most Important Skill" (*Forbes Magazine*, FEB15): www.forbes.com/sites/gregsatell/2015/02/06/why-communication-is-todays-most-important-skill/#11e0510c3638

Richard Branson: "Communication Is the Most Important Skill Any Leader Can Possess." (*Forbes Magazine*, JUL15): www.forbes.com/sites/carminegallo/2015/07/07/richard-branson-communication-is-the-most-important-skill-any-leader-can-possess/#7602dff74ff2

Anderson, Cushing and John F. Gantz (2013), "Skills Requirements for Tomorrow's Best Jobs: Helping Educators Provide Students with Skills and Tools They Need." Available at: https://news.microsoft.com/download/presskits/education/docs/IDC_101513.pdf

"Employers: Verbal Communication Most Important Candidate Skill." (National Association of Colleges and Employers, FEB16): www.naceweb.org/s02242016/verbal-communication-important-job-candidate-skill-aspx

If people are afraid to tell us what we need to hear, we will never hear unpleasant or bad information. That means that the "shoot the messenger" type of "leader" will only hear a small percentage of what they really need to hear in order to have awareness of the organization and of themselves as the leader.

A tendency to transmit does not guarantee that you will be a good communicator and a tendency to listen doesn't prevent you from being a good speaker either. The tendency is what we are most comfortable with and what we are naturally inclined to do – it doesn't preclude you from being good in the opposite tendency. In other words, quality of communications is a separate issue from the quantity or, in this case, the tendency in communications.

"We, Not I"

In November of 2002, my battalion and I were getting ready to deploy to Afghanistan for Operation Enduring Freedom. The fighting in Afghanistan had slowed down significantly as the Taliban and Al Qaeda slipped into the shadows to regroup and lick their wounds. That said, Afghanistan was (and still is) a dangerous place and a gun fight could happen anytime or place.

This was also before the invasion of Iraq and the overthrow of Saddam's regime in the spring of 2003. While we understood the concept of "winning hearts and minds," this was very much a combat operation we were training for.

Five months earlier, our parent headquarters, 3rd Brigade of the 82nd Airborne Division, deployed to Afghanistan with our two sister battalions and a battalion from 1st Brigade while we remained on two-hour alert as the Division Ready Force-1 for most of that time.[4] The biggest problem with being on "recall" all that time wasn't the requirement to be back at Fort Bragg within two hours; it was the inability to train while our equipment was locked up and prepared for an airborne operation.

That put us behind in our training so instead of taking the Veteran's Day weekend off like most of our sister battalions (we were now "attached" to 1st Brigade), we were conducting combat training on the ranges of Fort Bragg.

I was supervising what was essentially a company level live-fire exercise on one range while the other companies in the battalion did training

---

4. At that time, the 82nd Airborne had nine infantry battalions and they were numbered based on when they would deploy on little or no notice. While the standard for the Division Ready Force 1 (DRF-1) was to be "wheels-up" in eighteen hours from alert, that required that most of our equipment was prepped or rigged for parachute delivery and therefore not available for training. It also meant that all our soldiers had to stay close to Fort Bragg and be able to assemble within two hours of the alert.

elsewhere. This is why on the night of 9 November I was on Range 63 with Alpha Company while our Bravo Company was on Range 27 B.

Bravo Company was led by the best commander/first sergeant team that we had. They were innovators and challenged their team to be the best they could be at everything. Even with their talent and effort, there was a near-fatal accident on the range that night.

A young private from New York City, not naturally inclined to being in the woods at night with a gun, but motivated to serve after what happened to his city on 9/11, crossed in front of his team leader during the live fire and was shot from behind.

Nothing can erase or change how bad a thing that is to happen; shooting one of your own, especially in training is about as serious a mistake as you can make. But that said, everything that happened after that was about as perfect as it could have been and stands as a testament to how good we were as a team with regards to adaptability and influence.

Our medics were the best I'd ever seen, thanks in no small measure to our physician's assistant, George Barbee. He had our medics working to their highest level of competence because he focused on their purpose and he helped to develop their adaptability through building their confidence, initiative and accountability.

The wounded soldier was immediately treated and stabilized and the company called for an evacuation helicopter (there is always one on stand-by at Fort Bragg for just such an emergency). Within twelve minutes of the incident, the soldier was in the Emergency Department of Womack Army Medical Center and undergoing surgery.

We began the process to assess what went wrong that night immediately but also the process to heal and recover. Because I knew that his teammates would be devastated, I sent our battalion chaplain to help them deal with their concerns and potential feelings of guilt. We were lucky to have the best chaplain possible on our team at that time and I knew that Peter Dietsch would listen to the soldiers in Bravo Company and that he would know what to say to begin the healing process.

By morning, we had a pretty good idea of what happened if not why it happened and so my sergeant major and I went to see our boss. Because we were now a part of 1st Brigade, our boss was Colonel John Campbell. Of all the people I have worked for in my life, John Campbell was clearly in the top five. It says a lot about him that as I write this, he is the four-star general commanding all U.S. and NATO forces in Afghanistan.

I'm not sure what his natural tendencies were, probably because he seemed so skilled at finding balance with each situation. But I do believe that his natural tendency with communication is to receive. And so on the morning of 10 November, in a situation where my previous boss would have been yelling at me from the moment I entered his office, John Campbell asked me what happened on Range 27 B and he listened while we recounted the events before, during and after the point one of my soldiers had been shot.

What happened next will forever keep John Campbell in my personal "Pantheon of Heroes." The first words out of his mouth once we were done talking, and without a moment's hesitation, were: "Okay, here's what we need to do…"

I was floored. Not only by his example to listen, to stay with the receive tendency of communication, but when he did move to transmit, it was with exactly the right words. "We" is a powerful word; it expresses a sense of team but also a sense of ownership. John Campbell just took ownership, not only for finding a solution but for the problem. It wasn't a 2-Panter problem at that point but a 1st Brigade problem.

This may seem like a minor thing but believe me when I tell you that not every commander in his position would say or do what he just did. He let us know that we were in this together, that he had our back and it would always be so. We were about to go into combat and he probably understood that there would be times when his understanding of any situation would depend on the information he received from his subordinates. By taking ownership of a potentially career-ending situation like this, he probably knew that we would come to him in the future with bad news as much as we'd come to report good news.

What he told us amounted to getting to a better understanding of what happened on Range 27B, not to figure out whose head should be taken off but to know if what went wrong was systemic or unique; were there things we could learn to make us more effective in combat? Could this accident have been prevented and what could we do to prevent similar situations in the future?

So, he not only knew how to find balance between transmit and receive in communications, he knew what to say when he did transmit.

"We, not I" was one of the tenets I had learned from another great Army leader, LTG Bob Caslen.[5] John Campbell put that tenet into full effect that morning. By focusing on what we could learn from the accident and not who was to blame, he was trying to find the positive in a very negative situation. And that was a second tenet that I had learned long ago and tried to live every day: "Solutions, not blame." Unless negligence is involved, getting to a solution to a problem is always more important than assigning blame. I don't remember ever hearing John say those words exactly but he was certainly living them in how he communicated.

In the end, the soldier recovered from his wound but was not able to deploy and was later discharged. But as a team, we grew and came to some very fundamental understandings. We knew that when we needed to tell our boss something, no matter how bad, he would listen. It's always the boss's prerogative to answer or act how he/she wants but if you want to make sure you are being told all you need to know, not just what you want to hear, the leader needs to be receptive.

With leadership, the follow-up to listening is almost always going to be the transmission of some guidance or directive. What you say will always be more important than how much you say. "Okay, here's what we need to do..." preceded more detailed guidance and direction but those seven words set the tone for every bit of communication that ever occurred between me and my boss after that. It could have very easily gone in a totally different direction if Campbell had replaced the word "we" with the word "you."

The phrase "We, not I" reminds us to be humble and inclusive as a leader and unless there is a need for personal accountability as in "I messed that up" or "That was my fault," we works best in most situations. Another phrase, "we, not you," similarly puts the focus on team and shared accountability for events and results.

Self-Awareness

You Likely Have a Tendency to Transmit If:

- You speak freely and easily
- You don't listen well

---

5. LTG Robert "Bob" Caslen is currently Superintendent of the United States Military Academy. When he was the commander of 2nd Brigade of the 101st Airborne Division at Fort Campbell, KY, I had the honor to be his operations officer (S3).

- When someone else is talking, you focus on what you are going to say next
- People tell you what you want to hear, not what you need to hear

You Likely Have a Tendency to Receive If:

- You listen actively
- You think about what someone else has said before you reply or speak up
- You'd rather take notes during a briefing than give the briefing
- People tell you what you need to know, bad news as well as good news

We must first understand our true tendency in communications before we can do anything else because so much of our situational/environmental awareness is tied to what we receive (and perceive) about the environment. That requires us to both articulate what we need and are looking for or looking to accomplish as well as the ability to take in the necessary information.

What most often happens is that a person who is steadfastly a transmitter will miss cues and information from their boss, peers and subordinates. They will fail to know a large percentage of the information available to make a decision or to make good recommendations. Conversely, with the person who is steadfastly a receiver, they will not send out the messages and instructions they need their boss, peers or subordinates to know. There might be a qualitative aspect to this as well but often it is just a matter of not sending a signal at the right time to the right receiver.

So, what is your natural tendency?

Think for a moment about conversations you have every day with the people in your work environment. Do you find yourself thinking about what you are going to say next when they are talking? Do you enjoy being in the front of the room to brief a project? Do you find yourself asking people: "What did you just say?" or "Can you please repeat that?" Have you ever realized after the fact that people were withholding information from you; that they told you what they thought you wanted to hear, not what you needed to hear?

This last case is interesting because it speaks to how you react to information. When someone tells you something, it is an attempt to communicate where they are in transmission mode and you are in reception mode – or at least you should be in reception mode. However, if you are the kind of leader who reacts poorly to bad news or if you have ever "shot the messenger," it is highly likely that your natural tendency is to transmit, not receive.

Another classic example is when you don't really listen to what is being said but use that time instead to think about what brilliant or pithy thing you will say next. This is one of the most obvious indications of a tendency to transmit in a way that is well out of balance with your tendency to receive. Unfortunately, a true and honest self-assessment is the only way to uncover this tendency. It's possible that your tendency to think of your next signal is discernable to others but if that is the case, they will likely have a hard time telling you about it because you are probably not inclined to listen. And if you are a "shoot the messenger type," there is even less chance that they will attempt to communicate this insight with you.

There is a possible cross-over to the domain of focus here as well. If you have a tendency to be selfish, as well as a tendency to transmit, the two will compound each other.

Your tendencies might also be affected by the situation at hand. Do you receive better when you are in charge or the senior person in the room? Do you act differently when the boss is in the room? Either condition could cause you to move more towards transmit because you see your responsibility as the leader in the first case or because you are driven to impress in the second case.

Central to the tendency of transmit is a desire to get some fact, idea or opinion out into the world. You have something to say and you intend to say it. It would be great if you could temper that to only those things with impact and importance to your team and therein lies the art and science of achieving balance. As a leader, you must decide what is important and what other people must know too. The exclusive aspects of communication are that you decide what the message is and when, how and with whom to send it. That is the end state but before you get there, you have to have information and insights and this is where the inclusive part of communications comes in – you have to be receptive to all the information that is out there for you to consider. Sometimes that information sounds like a lot of noise and sometimes it comes from a source we might not consider important but it all begins with the reception of a message. The hardest message for us to understand and use is the one that we miss or, worse, the one that is never sent.

We often assign a virtuous quality to the tendency to receive: "God gave you one mouth and two ears; you should listen twice as much as you talk…" In general, that is a great rule to follow but as a leader you have to find balance with the situation and your tendency so that you can transmit or receive appropriately.

If you'd rather be the person on the team taking notes, you probably have a tendency to receive. If you ask questions (appropriately) to clarify someone else's message, you probably have a tendency to receive as well. Do you sit on information, waiting on confirmation or additional insights before you share this information with anyone else? If so, you might be an extreme receiver.

On the plus side, if people are open in telling you what they think you need to know, you are probably a natural receiver. This might also manifest itself as people coming to you with their personal problems. In a work environment, the former case is a very positive sign and indicator of the type of climate you have created and you are most certainly not a "shoot the messenger" type. The latter case could be a positive as well if it allows you to really know your team and understand what is going on in their lives that you can help them fix or deal with better. But what should one do with all the information that comes to a person or leader who is naturally receptive?

"Decisions are made in the absence of fact…"[6]

Decision making is a subject and a discipline unto itself but suffice it to say that one of the primary roles of the leader is to make decisions. If you possessed all (or perfect) information needed to make a decision, the best or correct choice would be obvious; in essence, there would be no need to make a decision – the facts would do that for you. However, in the real world, we never have all the information or perfect information so decisions must be made in the absence of (all the) facts. It is the inclusive domain of communications that allows us to gather facts and information, however complete or imperfect, and therefore it is essential to the quality and quantity of our transmissions in the exclusive domain of communications.

Situational Awareness

Do your people listen well? Do they understand what you are telling them? Do they provide you with the information you need? Do they know how

---

6. One of my first mentors, Lieutenant General Robert W. Wagner, was my company tactical officer at West Point when he was a major and I was a cadet. This quotation stuck with me because when he first said it, I didn't understand what it meant. On reflection, it became obvious: if you have all the facts, the decision makes itself.

you process information? While this is a question of the natural communication tendencies of you and your people, the quality of communications cannot be discounted when we begin to talk about the effectiveness of our communications. Therefore, in building your situational awareness for communications, it's not enough to understand your tendencies for communications and what is going on in your environment; you must also know how people learn and understand things.

How do the people on your team process information? Do they have the ability to provide you with information in the manner which you process it best? These two questions embody the essence of understanding whether we are talking about your ability to communicate (transmit and receive) effectively or your team's ability to communicate.

People process information in different ways; some of us are auditory and like hearing information; some of us are visual and like to see information; others of us are kinesthetic and need to touch or move with information; and some of us are a mix of these different styles. How we process information is closely tied to our learning style, which means that when we communicate with others, it's not our style that matters so much as the other person's.[7]

So, once you determine the individual and collective communication tendencies of your team, you need to figure out how best to transmit information. Equally as important, you need to make sure they know your processing style so that they can transmit information to you more effectively.

If you are in balance regarding communications, there will be a constant and effective flow of information and understanding. When information is not getting to the right people or if it is lost in transmission or translation, you and your team have a problem and that problem is most likely due to an imbalance regarding communications.

The easy answer to explain an imbalance in communications is that you either have a problem with transmission or reception – but which tendency is it and with whom? Is the problem with you or with the team? Again, we could talk volumes about your relationship with your boss and other stakeholders in your environment, but for now, in this book, we will focus on you and the team you lead.

Like the warden in the movie *Cool Hand Luke* starring Paul Newman, just saying, "We seem to have a failure to communicate..." is only a starting

---

7. http://www4.ncsu.edu/unity/lockers/users/f/felder/public/ILSdir/styles.htm

point. Getting at the problem requires self-awareness of you and your communication tendency as well as that of your team. Because you are one and the team can be many, the greater burden will be on you when it comes to adjusting to individual communication and learning styles but that's why you are the leader and it's ultimately your responsibility to make it all work.

Strategies for Being the Fulcrum with Communications

- Learn and practice active listening skills
- When you receive some new information or when analysis of old information leads you to some new understanding, the first question you should ask is: "Who else needs to know?..."
- Learn and practice feedback skills in the form of an "immediate brief-back"
- Find your "Napoleon's Corporal"
- Know how you process information; do the same with the members of your team
- Focus on quality of communications first, quantity second
- Pay attention to nonverbals

Active Listening

The term "active listening" was first used by Thomas Gordon in his 1977 book *Leader Effectiveness Training*. "Active listening is certainly not complex. Listeners need only restate, in their own language, their impression of the expression of the sender. ... Still, learning to do Active Listening well is a rather difficult task."[8]

What makes it a difficult task, in my mind, is that it requires more effort and, if not done well, makes the active listener come across as rude. I also think that there is a natural hesitancy for anyone in a junior position to do this with a senior ranking person. More on that later but both you and the people on your team would do well to get comfortable with active listening.

The keys here are first that the listener – receiver really because we communicate with more than just words and sounds – is actively involved in the communication, not passive to the sounds or images presented to him/her. Second, that person receiving the communications must restate the message in their own words. Now it's not just "parroting" what the transmitter just

8. Gordon, Thomas (1977), *Leader Effectiveness Training*. New York: Wyden Books. (p. 57.ISBN 0-399-12888-3.)

said but it is a statement of understanding as in "this is what I thought I heard you say..." More on this later with the brief-back and Napoleon's corporal but the point here is that it's not enough to repeat the communication; you must demonstrate your understanding of it back to the transmitter.

More than any other technique, this will serve you well in finding balance and effectiveness in your communications.

"Who Else Needs to Know?"

This is the mantra of anyone who has served on a staff in the military. The primary job of staff officers is to gather information, analyze it and then make a recommendation to the commander. What often happens is that people focus on their own little area of expertise and "stove pipe" information. Usually, information flows well in a vertical direction but not horizontally, hence the reference to a stovepipe or silo.

Effective staff officers break out of the vertical flow of information by asking the simple question, "Who else needs to know...?" While the answer may in fact be "no one else needs to know" and within the intelligence community, this is often the culture. For the rest of us, however, where success is based on more people knowing what's going on, it is more about filling in the parts of the puzzle. Often, we don't have a full idea of the importance or impact of some bit of information so we don't share it. But if we take a moment to ask if anyone else should have or could do some more analysis with this information, we should share it.

This simple act of thinking about and directing information to other people who might need it forces us to move from a primarily passive role as a receiver of information to an active transmitter of information. It is in itself an act of finding balance in your communications and it has the potential to make any organization much more efficient and connected.

Your job as the leader is to recognize when there is "stove piping" going on in your organization. Let your team know that you want them to practice the tenet of "who else needs to know" and then incentivize the practice of shared understanding by your example and by praising it when it happens.

Brief-back

Another trick of the trade that I learned in my years as a soldier is something called the "immediate brief-back." This is a technique to ensure that subordinate commanders understand the commander's intent. It is very similar to active listening but it serves the function to confirm one's understanding of a specific task.

The brief-back needs to become part of the culture within your organization if it's going to work. It then becomes one of the foundations for a more indirect style of influence as the members of your team take ownership for their tasks and duties. When your people are able to tell you in their own words what they have been tasked to do and why they need to do it – purpose – your team will improve exponentially. I'll talk about this more when we get to influence as a domain but it starts with how and how well you and your team communicate.

For example, if I give you a task to reorganize your department to be more accessible to our customers, you would immediately tell me in your own words the task (reorganize the department) and the purpose (greater accessibility to customers) with some of the detail of how you intend to do it. That way I can confirm your understanding and you can move forward in complete confidence that we are both clear on what needs to be done. This facilitates what we could call "shared understanding" of the task. It might take you and your team a little bit of time to get into the habit of doing back-briefs because it may seem as if trust is an issue. Trust is an issue but in this case it is improved through shared understanding, not diminished because the boss demands a briefing on assigned tasks.

Napoleon's Corporal

When I was a cadet at West Point studying military history, one of my professors told the story of Napoleon's corporal. Napoleon was one of the greatest military minds of all time (he was also a tyrant who named himself Emperor of France but that's another story).

Napoleon knew that few in his army were as brilliant or gifted in the art and science of war as he was. In fact, he knew that success or failure in battle was often the result of how well the common soldier could execute his great plans. It is also true that most of his army were not professionals but average citizens pulled from farms and villages and cities from all across France. For these reasons, Napoleon knew that he needed a failsafe way to ensure that instructions he gave to his staff were clearly articulated in written orders that the army would execute.

As the story goes, Napoleon picked a corporal out of the ranks of his massive army. The corporal was a step above a private, a leader of men but at the level of most direct action – the tip of the spear as the saying goes. It was important that the corporal could read, but again, this was a soldier from the front lines, not a General or Marshall of France.

Napoleon would have the corporal read the orders that his staff produced for the coming battle. Then he would have the corporal (in his own words) tell Napoleon what the plan for battle was. If the corporal's understanding of the plan was exactly as Napoleon intended, the plan was ready for the staff to issue. If, however, the corporal's understanding was in any way off from Napoleon's intent, he would send the order back to the staff with instructions for them to re-write the portion that the corporal didn't clearly understand as Napoleon envisioned. On and on this process would continue until Napoleon was hearing from the corporal exactly what he intended and how the order should be written.

I love this story. I mentioned it once to some French officers I was training for a deployment to Afghanistan and they had never heard of it before. They looked at me like I was crazy; they had never heard of this communications technique and they didn't seem to hold Napoleon in the same regard that I did. No matter, whether a true story or some exaggerated tale, it exemplifies much of the concept for finding balance in your communications. You can do this with everyone on your team, or depending on the size of your team, pick one or two people to serve in this role as "Napoleon's corporal" to give you feedback on the clarity of your instructions and directives.

This story also highlights that Napoleon probably understood the learning style and level of his team, both the soldiers on the front lines and the staff doing the plans and orders. He knew that he had to listen to what people thought they understood of his communications and intentions. His process was both active and passive and reflected an ability to find balance between the transmit and the receive tendencies of communications.

Learning Styles

That story becomes a great place to mention learning styles. Why do we need to talk about learning styles? Think about what it means to learn. Learning is the act of processing information in order to develop a new skill or to retain some bit of knowledge. We form teams to accomplish things and that usually requires skill or knowledge or both. This is why communicating works best when we understand how members of our team (including you, the leader) process information.

Some of the experts in this field will parse learning styles all the way down to seven or eight different categories, taking into account if the learner is social or solitary or differentiating music from other sounds but for my purposes and for this book, I will use the VARK method developed by Neil D. Fleming. VARK is an acronym for visual, auditory, read/write and kinesthetic and Fleming developed an assessment tool to identify an individual's preference for receiving and transmitting information.[9]

Much like our tendency in the four domains of Fulcrum-centric Leadership, many of us have a preference to learn by either seeing pictures or diagrams (visual), hearing sounds (auditory), reading or writing out instructions, or finally by touching or moving (kinesthetic). Fleming also recognizes that some people are "multi-modal" in that their preference is a combination of any two or more of the four styles.

The point of all this is that effective communications and effective learning both can hinge on how the information is presented or received. If a member of your team is an auditory learner and you hand her a technical manual, she is probably going to have a hard time learning about the new equipment you want her to become expert on. An audio book would be better for her.

You might want to consider having the members of your team take the VARK survey so that you can better understand how they learn and therefore the best ways to communicate with them. While you are at it, make sure you understand your learning style so your team can provide you with the information you need in the style that best suits your preference for processing and learning.[10]

Therefore, being the fulcrum with your team may involve not only shifting whether you transmit or receive but how you communicate. Understanding the learning style of the people you work with can be a great aid in both how you transmit and receive information.

As an example, you might be primarily auditory in how you process information but the graphic artists on your team are predominantly visual and kinesthetic. This might require you to learn how to make rough diagrams of the things you want or need them to do (transmission) or learn how to interpret their designs.

---

9. Fleming, Neil D. (2001), *Teaching and Learning Styles: VARK Strategies*
10. http://vark-learn.com/the-vark-questionnaire/

At this point, I think it's safe to equate a learning style with a communications style. If you cannot communicate in another person's style, you might as well be speaking a foreign language. That leaves you with one of three options: 1) learn how to communicate in other styles – in essence, you become multi-lingual; 2) get an interpreter to help you understand through translation; and 3) blow it all off and fail to communicate.

Finally, and in line with communications styles, is the means to communicate. You'll see this in your work environment in that some people need and want face-to-face communications. Others, either because of their preference or because of their location, prefer some means of technology. If they are auditory, call them; if they are read/write in their style, send an email; if they are visual, send a picture by email. You get the point but it's on you to figure out what works best in each situation.

And the very last thing I'll say about this is culture matters. If you are working across international, gender or age boundaries, take that into consideration too. Famously, millennials respond best to texting over email – that's certainly the case with my youngest son. Recognize that you might have a boundary and learn what works on the other side or get a guide to help you.

Quality, Not Quantity

While these methods to find balance in the communications domain address the types of interactions you have with your team, it's important to remember that quality trumps quantity all the time. The essence of the active listening and the other techniques I offer here is that they will help you with the quality of your communications in both transmission and reception. Keep that in mind as you become the fulcrum in the communications domain.

A Word about Nonverbals

I am the furthest thing from an expert on body language and non-verbal communication but I know enough to understand that it matters.

With over thirty-four million views, it's highly likely you've seen Amy Cuddy's TED talk.[11] While the theme of her talk is about power dynamics and how our body position affects how we feel, there can also be a significant impact on communications. Does your posture facilitate or exacerbate your

11. http://www.ted.com/talks/amy_cuddy_your_body_language_shapes_who_you_are

ability to transmit or receive? I'm certain of its importance and it's worth making that part of your self-awareness. Cuddy calls it "presence" and describes how it affects the way you see yourself and the way the world sees you.[12] If that's not communicating, I'm not sure what is.

So, how you present yourself physically or virtually will certainly affect your ability to communicate be it in the transmit or the receive side of the domain. Take that into consideration and always, always, always look people in the eye when you are talking with them.

If you are transmitting an idea, looking the other person(s) in the eye allows them to connect more personally with you and if you are receiving, you will be able to convey your level of understanding as well as your commitment and interest in what they are sending. There is no one better way to communicate without speaking.

SUMMARY

- Know your tendency
- Understand what the situation demands right now: Is there some information you need others to know or do you need to receive more information from the environment?
- Listen actively
- Figure out who else "needs to know"
- Get comfortable giving feedback; get your team good at it too by being receptive to it
- Find your "corporal" to assess the clarity of the message and how it is interpreted
- Understand that how people process information affects communications; know your learning style and the styles of your team
- Focus on the quality of communications, not the quantity; they are not the same thing
- Pay attention to non-verbal communications

To learn more or to continue this conversation, go to www.bethefulcrum.com where you can find additional content or get help with your specific leadership development needs.

12. Cuddy, Amy (2015), *Presence: Bringing Your Boldest Self to Your Biggest Challenges*, Little Brown and Company, ISBN 978-0-316-25657-5

ADAPTABILITY

Adaptability

Adaptable: *adjective* adapt·able \a-'dap-ta-bal, a-\

: Able to change or be changed in order to fit or work better in some situation or for some purpose; able to adapt or be adapted[13]

Adaptability Defined

While not a part of this definition, we often think of adaptability and leadership with regards to creativity in decision making or problem solving. I agree with that association . At least, it's been my experience that adaptive leaders are better problem solvers, better able to deal with the unknown or chaos, conditions that soldiers face on a daily basis.

The U.S. Army Asymmetric Warfare Group recognized this as well and developed a training program called the Asymmetric Warfare Adaptive Leader Program or AWALP for short. AWALP was a product of years spent working with soldiers in something called Outcomes-Based Training and Education (OBTE). OBTE recognized that in a complex and ambiguous

---

13. http://www.merriam-webster.com/dictionary/adaptability

battlefield environment, soldiers needed to be focused more on outcomes and results than on process and procedures – this ran counter to nearly two centuries of precedent for training soldiers to fight industrial age warfare.

"Wait, you want soldiers to think and be creative; to use their initiative?" What would Baron Friedrich von Steuben say about that idea? Von Steuben was a Prussian (German) born general who established a standardized training program for the Continental Army of George Washington. He is considered a founding father of the United States Army. Based on the tactics of the day, his job was to train citizen-soldiers the basics of standing, firing and reloading their muskets as they stood fifty meters across from a professional enemy force doing the same thing. As A.J. Langguth describes in his wonderful book *Patriots*, "Writing to a friend in Europe, he (von Steuben) noted that with Prussians, Austrians or Frenchmen you say to your soldier, 'Do this,' and he does it, but I am obliged to say, 'This is the reason you ought to do that.' And then he (the American soldier) does it"[14] So, it seems that even back in 1778, American soldiers needed to know the reason why they should do something. That said, for most of our history, soldiers and workers in general were expected to do what they were told.

At nearly every level of command, soldiers were expected to execute the orders they were given in a mission statement that contained five "W's". "You (Who), go do this thing (What), at this location (Where), at this time (When) for this purpose (Why)…" The emphasis was almost always on the first four "W's" of that mission statement: Who, What, Where and When. That last "W", "Why" was there to allow for controlled or measured initiative by a subordinate that saw a way to get the same outcome with a different what, where or when. Often we paid lip service to that concept of initiative but the Army and business seem to have gotten better about that in recent years – more on the subject when we talk about influence.

So, using AWALP and OBTE (later OBTE became Adaptive Soldier, Leader Training and Education or ASLTE) as an example, we see adaptability as an important domain for all soldiers but particularly for all soldiers who are leaders. But how to become more adaptive?

AWALP showed that you cannot do adaptability training but you can do training that enhances (or, if done wrong, destroys) adaptability. Training and educating soldiers and leaders with knowledge, skills and abilities

14. Langguth, A.J. (1988), *Patriots: The Men Who Started the American Revolution*, pg. 470, Simon & Schuster Paperbacks, ISBN-13: 978-0-671-67562-2(Pbk.)

needed to perform while at the same time developing the key attributes of confidence, initiative, accountability, decision making and problem solving is the path to greater adaptability.[15]

Using the same concepts in business is possible if you are willing to let people push to the edge of failure and to engage in opportunities to build confidence, initiative and accountability in their work. This involves an element of risk and resource management because in business you don't always have the luxury of keeping training separate from operations; opportunities to develop your people have to happen in the context of product delivery to a customer and can impact the top and bottom line negatively if done poorly.

AWALP is a great program and I couldn't agree more with its concepts for developing greater adaptability. It seems reasonable that most leaders and managers would see the value in a program that fosters those key attributes on the way to a more adaptable worker or team. But even people who can embrace this concept can get stuck on the decision making part of leadership/management.

As we discussed earlier with the role of communications, decision making and judgment are components of management and leadership. This is why we pay managers, executives and leaders the big bucks: not just to make decisions but to make sound, wise and good decisions. But decision making by itself is an insufficient way to look at this domain of leadership and the primary reason why I use adaptability as the second domain in Fulcrum-centric Leadership. What makes adaptability a more essential domain is that it deals with the front-side of decision making (how and why you make a decision) and it also addresses the back-side of decision making: when, how and why to change a decision you made previously.

So again, we often focus on decision making and judgment in how leaders solve problems as if it were a static thing. But just as Newton informs our understanding of physics: that for every action, there is an equal and opposite reaction (Third Law of Motion), so too in leadership, with every action (decision) there is some reaction – not necessarily equal or opposite. With this in mind, why do we not spend more time looking at follow-through on decisions? If it takes judgment to make a decision in the first place, what does it take to recognize that a decision wasn't the best (or even a good) decision?

---

15. "AWG Leader's Guide for Enhancing Adaptability, Version 2," December 2011.

Adaptability is an important leadership domain for making decisions but it is equally, if not more important, in assessing the validity of our decisions. More often than not a decision is not good or bad – but rather right or wrong – based on what we do after the decision has been made. This follow-through is what gets many leaders into trouble. They might stick with a decision no matter what, even in the face of evidence that it was the wrong choice. They might change a decision too quickly at the first sign of trouble. How do we prevent either of these two conditions as a leader? Whether it is pride or incompetence that causes this matters little; what is important is an understanding of this tendency and looking for the indicators that a fulcrum shift is needed.

The ability to recognize and adapt to the situation is just as important after a decision has been made as it is before a decision is made. The environment will always change as a reaction to our decisions, which means that decision making is a fluid process, not a static process. That means the leader must be willing to look for evidence that it was a bad decision or that factors have changed and now she needs to do something different or counter to the first move.

It been my experience, however, that many leaders are too rigid in their thinking; even though they may recognize the problem(s) with their decisions, something prevents them from doing anything about it. That something is usually their rigid tendency in the adaptability domain.

"Getting Left of Boom"

In 2004, with combat operations shifting to an unconventional fight in Iraq, the United States and coalition forces started seeing more and more of what are known as Improvised Explosive Devices or IEDs. While most of this same coalition had been in Afghanistan since 2001, the use of IEDs was not as common – but that would change over time. Essentially a "road-side bomb," the enemies we faced – they were not all part of the same team or even the same ideology but the one thing they had in common was a desire to kill Americans – became very adapt in developing new ways to build, hide, trigger and even deliver these weapons of death and destruction. We started referring to the use of IEDs as an asymmetric threat: something that is very different from the way we fight (or more importantly, the way we want to fight). The key issue here is that asymmetric threats and asymmetric warfare aren't so much about what someone does to us but really about our ability (or inability) to effectively deal with and beat that threat.

As more and more soldiers were being killed and wounded by IEDs, the U.S. Army realized that it was facing a threat it was not equipped to defeat or even to understand. Fortunately for the Army, Peter J. Schoomaker had accepted the request to come out of retirement and took over as the 35th Chief of Staff of the Army in 2003. Schoomaker had previously served as commander of the Joint Special Operations Command and the United States Special Operations Command so his background was in both conventional (he started his Army career as an armor officer) and unconventional warfare.

Schoomaker realized the need for something different to face this "new" threat so he created a new organization that was chartered to look at the problem and develop solutions. That organization was called the IED Task Force.[16]

In another stroke of genius or luck, a new one-star general named Joe Votel was selected to form and command this new task force. Votel was able to assemble a talented group, including a select group of contractors; all retired Army Special Operators from The Wexford Group International.

With this dream team of talent, the IED Task Force began to work with Army units in Iraq. They saw firsthand what was working and what was not working. They realized early on that most units were very passive in how they approached the enemy and this new threat: they drove their vehicles until they were blown up and then they reacted. Now, reacting to an ambush is a battle drill all combat units practice for good reason but if you want to win in combat, in sports and in life, at some point you have to go on offense and score more points than your opponent.

The Army in general, and most units serving in Iraq specifically, were playing defense and while a good defense is key to victory, without offense, the best you can hope for is a tie. Put another way, and in the words of General George Patton, the best defense is a good offense. It was obvious in the "Sanford and Son"[17] armor being applied by units in the field that we needed a solution but the lack of proactive steps to defeat the insurgents using the IEDs meant that we could hope for little more than a draw.

Votel and the task force realized that to defeat the IEDs, Army units needed to play offense and defense; they had to be able to stop the attacks before

---

16. Later, the IED Task Force became the Joint IED Task Force in order to provide solutions to the other services, primarily the Marine Corps. The Army decided to retain its own capability so the Joint IED Task Force became two separate organizations: The Joint IED Defeat Organization, or JIEDDO, and the Army Asymmetric Warfare Group, or AWG.

17. From the TV sitcom of the 1970s about a junkyard owner and his son; units were welding armor plates, taken from damaged vehicles or found in various junkyards, to protect their "thin-skin" vehicles.

they happened as well as survive the attacks when they did happen. This required a new way of thinking and acting; of seeing the enemy and the way "he" operated as a network and seeing the network as something you could attack. This required better understanding of how the bad guys worked and better intelligence on where and when they were doing all the steps needed to put a bomb in the ground and blow up a passing truck.

With this concept in mind, Votel understood that it wouldn't be enough to develop this adaptive way of thinking and acting. He needed a way to explain it to soldiers and commanders so they would embrace the method and start to play offense as well as defense.

This is where communications and influence come into play as well. Votel and the task force had their own thoughts and ideas about the problem and the solutions but they first went out to receive as much information as possible. Units had to transmit what was going on but there was not collective analysis across the entire theater of operations. Votel knew too that whatever solutions the task force recommended, if units didn't believe in their effectiveness or feel a sense of ownership, they were likely to stick with the reactionary method of dealing with the problem.

So, the task force developed a graphic to show what was going on. Across a horizontal axis, they listed all the activities that go into an IED attack. Starting on the left with planning for the attack and moving across with building the device and conducting reconnaissance, to the actual attack and then escaping to do it all over again on the right, these events can take months or days on the far left down to minutes and seconds on the far right. Where the attack happened, Votel and his staff placed a cartoon-like explosion symbol with the word "BOOM" written on it.

Along a vertical axis, Votel listed the levels of "detectability" or how easy it is to see the enemy doing this. Across the graph, he then applied thresholds of detectability and engagement for each activity.

GETTING LEFT OF BOOM

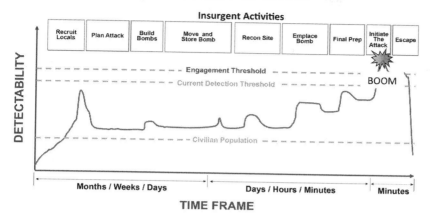

No matter what the activity, the population usually had a low threshold of detectability; in other words, the civilians living in the area saw or were aware of most IED activities. When they only reacted to the attack itself, soldiers had a very high threshold of detectability, meaning that they never saw the enemy until after the bomb exploded. Add to this the fact that soldiers must have positive identification of a threat and the intent to do harm before they can shoot at an enemy. We call this the rules of engagement or ROE and it's why convoys couldn't just go around shooting up everything that looked different or dangerous.

Here's what was going on. The bad guys were doing all this stuff to attack our vehicles with bombs. It would take months, weeks or days from start to finish and the civilians would know about most of it while it was going on in their neighborhoods. Local civilians saw the entirety of the activities on the chart from left to right.

In contrast, our soldiers that were in a reactive mode would only see the enemy and his actions when the bomb exploded way over on the right side of the chart. In typical fashion for the Army at the time, the bomb was the problem but not just the bomb – it was the bomb blowing up our vehicles. Certainly, the solution was with a better, bigger, more heavily armed vehicle. It worked in the past so it must be the solution now...

Votel and his team saw the problem differently and, laid out on this chart, it became obvious what we needed to do. Soldiers and units needed to get active within communities to develop contacts and gain their trust and confidence so the locals would tell them where the bombs were being made, stored and who was doing it. Once that happened, units could use that information to act and attack the network of bomb makers before they had a chance to blow up a convoy or a group of soldiers.

The problem wasn't the bomb or our vehicles; the problem was the network of insurgents using the bomb.

Figuratively (looking at the graph) and literally (on the ground), it was clear that to survive and win, we needed to move away from only seeing and engaging the enemy on the right side of the chart. We had to do the things that would get us the information to see and understand the network and then we had to attack it during those earlier activities on the left and center of the chart.

We had to get "left of BOOM."

It was pure genius. It communicated in a simple and clear way what the real problem was and options for how to solve it. It allowed for innovation among soldiers and units and it instilled confidence in our troops that there was a way to win.

Votel and his team recognized that as an organization, the Army in Iraq had a tendency to keep doing the same thing. Most units were rigid in their approach to the enemy and the fight, relying on what had worked in the past – superior firepower and heavy armor – to solve this new problem.

The IED Task Force saw the situation and realized that they had to help the individual soldiers and collective units be more flexible in seeing the problem and solving it. At that time, most units in the Army were pretty rigid in how they approached the IED problem because they didn't have the mindset or the resources (it seemed) to do more than react to the bomb after it went off. That's was a big IFK but with the help of the IED Task Force and this concept of getting left of boom, most units did restore balance in adaptability.

While the military continued to build bigger and heavier vehicles to protect soldiers, it took on a new attitude as well, not only about the enemy but about the civilian population. Much of the current doctrine for counter insurgency (COIN in military terms) stems from this idea that the people see and know more of what is going on in their communities and to get them to work with you, you need to develop their trust and confidence.

In 2004, that was a very new and different way of thinking. Votel and the IED Task Force could have been rigid in their thinking and with their solutions and it would probably have been sufficient to save some lives. But the situation required a more flexible mindset and more flexible solutions. "Getting left of boom" was so effective in moving the fulcrum in the fight against the insurgents in Iraq that it almost became cliché; people were using the term without any real understanding of its origins or the graphic that inspired the term. But even without that specific history, the term clarified (communications) and inspired (influence) a necessary change in action.

Self-Awareness

You Have a Tendency to Be Rigid If:
- You hate to (or cannot) admit you made a mistake
- Once you make a decision, you stick with it, no matter what
- You look for confirmation that you made the right/best decision
- You see everything in the world as either "black" or "white"
- You order the same thing off the menu
- You measure performance against an absolute standard

You Have a Tendency to Be Flexible If:
- You can and do admit when you've made a mistake
- You can change course or decisions if you see a better way
- You look for confirmation that you possibly didn't make the right/best decision
- You see shades of gray between the "black" and the "white"
- You are always looking for something new to try in a restaurant
- You measure performance against a relative standard

While I think that most people would agree that being more adaptable is better than being less adaptable, that's not the same thing as saying that there are times when you should be flexible and times when you should be rigid.

Take as a prime example the quotation:

> "In matters of style, swim with the current; in matters of principle, stand like a rock."
> ~ Thomas Jefferson

Sage advice from our third president but it assumes that you know when you ought to be swimming and when you ought to stand. That's situational awareness and we'll get there shortly but first we have to lock down our tendency. This is critical with adaptability because in my mind, this is where your IFK will really take over and cause you problems. And again, it's not just the initial decisions you make or how you solve problems; it's what you do to make sure that was/is a good decision down the road.

This is why your ability to admit a mistake is a key indicator for your adaptability tendency. Often, we can recognize that we made the wrong choice or even a bad choice but for many of us, it's nearly impossible to admit it. Why? The simple answer is pride but it's really a problem when pride and rigid combine to create a RFIFK (Really Fat Inner Fat Kid).

So, if your tendency is rigid and you are prideful, here's what's likely to happen sooner or later: BAM! That's the sound of your adaptability IFK slamming everything to the ground. At that point, it doesn't really matter if you recognize the mistake or not. The result is the same – you are immovable at the far end of the seesaw while the rest of your team is up in the air, feet dangling and the game comes to a grinding halt.

Think back to times when you were wrong. Even if that's a rare occasion, certainly we've all been wrong once or twice or hundreds of times before. How hard was it for you to admit you were wrong? It's critical that you are honest with yourself or else you'll never be able to accurately assess your tendency and then you'll never be able to be the fulcrum.

If it was easy to admit your mistake or that you were wrong, you likely have a tendency to be flexible. Likewise, if it was hard to admit you were wrong, you likely have a tendency to be rigid. There, not so hard to do, right? And the good news is that it doesn't matter so long as you can learn to be the fulcrum.

Closely related to admitting a mistake is the ability to change a decision you've made. As the "decider," you've put some thought and consideration into your decisions, or maybe not so much, but either way it's your decision so it must be brilliant…

This is what I know about decision making: if you are the type of person who makes a decision and moves on, never to look back, you probably have a rigid tendency for adaptability. If on the other hand, you make a decision but constantly look for a better or different course to take, you likely have a flexible tendency.

Here again we need to be careful not to assign a positive or negative quality to either tendency. As I've described the tendency for rigid (a term we tend to think of negatively) in the example above, we might relate that to decisiveness (a term we tend to think of positively). The same holds true with the example for flexibility; by itself flexibility usually holds a positive meaning but in the example above it could be taken as a sign of indecision or vacillation, two words with generally negative meanings.

Let me stress again here because this offers a great example. The tendencies in and of themselves are neither positive nor negative; it's only when we apply them to a given situation that their effect is either positive or negative. Understanding that and knowing how to be the fulcrum will allow you to turn any leadership situation from a negative to a positive.

What are some other indicators of your adaptability tendency? One indication of a rigid or flexible tendency is what you do look for in the aftermath of a decision.

If you are tending towards rigidity, you only look for evidence that you made the correct decision but if you are tending towards flexibility, you look for evidence that you make the incorrect decision. This is a form of confirmation bias: a tendency to look for the information that reinforces your beliefs and to discount information that doesn't reinforce your beliefs. This can happen as we gather information to make a decision as well as when we are looking to validate our choices. The rigid tendency will prevent us from seeing things we might need to see but don't because they reflect negatively on our decisions. The flexible tendency will allow us to look for positive and negative information but in doing so, we might be overwhelmed by the volume of knowledge.

If you have a tendency for flexibility, you likely see shades of gray while someone with a tendency for rigidity will only see "black" and "white." The distinction here is not insignificant and depending on your perspective you probably see one as positive and the other as negative. We might also say that seeing only "black" or "white" is binary: on or off; right or wrong; zero or one. With a rigid tendency, things are very clearly one thing or the opposite. The flexible tendency allows one to see the shades of gray between black and white. If you can rationalize varying degrees of good or bad, right or wrong, you are seeing shades of gray and likely have a tendency for flexibility in the adaptability domain.

"Black and white" or shades of gray relates to how we set standards for ourselves or for others but I'll use the terms absolute and relative as they relate to the tendency.

If you hold yourself to an absolute standard, you will not settle for something less. It doesn't matter what anyone else is doing or how much better you are than your peers; fail to meet the absolute standard and you've failed, no matter how good the result is. Absolute is the standard of someone with a rigid tendency. When looking at things in the world, the person with a rigid tendency is likely to see success and failure as a line to be crossed or a level to reach.

This is vastly different from a person with a flexible tendency because she will see success and failure relative to what else is going on in the world: "We didn't achieve our goal but we were 10% better than last year; that's pretty good…" "Our mutual fund lost 6% this year but most of our competitors lost 20-30%." Never mind that you lost money (most of us would agree that losing money is a bad thing), the fact that you lost much less than other people is relatively good. Success and failure are not based on a line you cross but where your finish line is compared to someone or something else.

Another indicator of your adaptability tendency can be seen in how you order in a restaurant. It could be any restaurant but let's say it's your favorite restaurant. If you order the same thing, all the time, you likely have a tendency to be rigid. If, however, you always try something different, you probably have a tendency to be flexible. Don't kid yourself into thinking you are flexible if you always order the chef's special but the chef only uses salmon in his specials; you have a rigid tendency because different ways to prepare salmon is still salmon.

Situational Awareness

When does the situation dictate more flexibility and when does it dictate a rigid adherence to a concept or a decision?

We can go back to Jefferson's quotation for advice. If we are dealing with core values – your personal values or the values of your team or company – it's safe to say that rigid is the tendency you need to exhibit and inforce. If you have a client, a customer or a teammate that just can't live with your values, your only option might be to lose them as a client or teammate. If your boss is the problem, you might have to find a new company to work for or have a conversation with your Human Resources director.

If, however, we are talking about trivial issues that have no bearing on our principles or values, say for instance the color of paper cups in the break room, it's quite possible that a flexible tendency is the way to go in order to find the best option or the newest way to do something. But these examples lie close to the extreme ends of the spectrum. Difficulty in seeing the situation happens mostly in the middle ground between the extremes.

So, if it's not clearly a case of swimming in the current of style (flexible) or standing on the rock of principle (rigid), how do you determine what tendency the situation requires?

The intended outcomes are the most important thing to consider when making a decision or when assessing the situation created by our actions and decisions. How do you achieve 'X' such thing or 'Y' results? The best approach might be the "tried and true" approach, something you and your team have done one hundred times in the past. But if the necessary outcome is something new and different, a new and different approach is likely your best bet but in the universe of new and different ideas, how do you decide which to take?

Time is therefore the second most important situational factor to consider for finding the right balance in adaptability. How much time do you have to make a decision? How much time to achieve your desired outcome? How much time to test your theories and change to Plan B? Certainly, more time can allow for greater flexibility while less time may drive you towards greater rigidity.

The third factor to consider in the situation is what resources, besides time, do you have at your disposal? Are you operating in a resource constrained environment or do you have unlimited resources? Are there other places you can go to for help? Can you outsource any part of this? In a situation where you lack resources, you might need to be more creative but you might also have to stand firmly on how, when and where those resources are deployed. With greater resources, there are likely more opportunities to be flexible but you have to be careful here to keep your people from thinking that they can waste or squander resources.

That last caveat is a reminder that either tendency can quickly move from a positive to a negative if it goes too far or doesn't keep pace with a changing situation.

Strategies for Being the Fulcrum with Adaptability

- Know what you believe in; what are your core values?
- Know what you are trying to accomplish; what will it look like when you are done?
- Know how much time you have to achieve the desired outcome
- Consider the longer term effects of your decisions, not just the immediate; where is the greatest impact?
- Don't wait for perfect information or all the facts to decide
- Be open to the possibility that you are equally wrong as you are right; look for indications of both once you have made a decision
- Look for sufficient evidence of the outcome, not perfect evidence. What are the indicators of success? What are the indicators of failure?
- Have alternative plans ready
- Visualize each plan and how the environment and the situation will change

Know Your Values

It's really as simple as the quotation from Jefferson: can you distinguish your core values, principles and beliefs from things that really don't matter or things that are a passing fad? If you haven't gone through this drill before, now is as good a time to start as any.

You can begin with a personal mission statement and outline what your purpose is in life. Why are you doing what you are doing and what do you intend to accomplish? This gives you your direction and end state so you should probably consider what that means for different time horizons like one year, five years and twenty years.

Next you should list the three to five values that you would never compromise. If they don't support your personal mission, you probably need to reevaluate your mission or look more closely at this value and decide if it is really essential to your core beliefs.

Next you need to check your values against those that are stated or acted out by your team and your organization. If all are in alignment, your only job is to keep them that way with consistent action, words and deeds. But, if your team or your company doesn't share your values, you have a much bigger problem and a much more important decision to make and that is: can you continue to work with these people?

Regardless, now that you have listed your values, you can check for them in your leadership situations concerning adaptability. If the situation involves one of the core principles, a rigid tendency is called for and if the situation doesn't involve a core principle, greater flexibility is not only called for, it is probably demanded. One caution here; don't assume that matters of "style" or anything not involving your principles will be trivial. Some of these issues will involve changes that allow greater innovation or that spark a new energy in your team.

Certainly issues of religion or politics that find their way into the work place could be one significant reason for incompatible values, but it could also be an issue of how customers are treated or how employees are treated. And it doesn't have to be an issue of legality, simply a difference in how you view relationships could be the cause of a values divide between you and your employer or boss.

Know Your Desired Outcome

This becomes an important part of adaptability when you consider not only what you want to accomplish but what do you want your team to learn? Do you see opportunities for growth and accountability?

If you have the chance to accomplish a task and use it as a way to grow greater initiative in your team, a flexible tendency is probably called for. Perhaps this is a new skill or a new method of operations and, in allowing for greater flexibility, you will achieve outcomes that you could never have anticipated. This generally spins off new initiatives and allows your team to grow as individuals and collectively.

If, on the other hand, your desired outcome is something routine or an intermediate step in a bigger process, a rigid tendency could be the most appropriate. This usually happens when process or quality involves specific and exacting standards. In these cases, an attempt to be flexible will likely cost more resources than you should or can spend in the name of innovation, learning or accountability.

We see this most often when someone wants to be innovative with a process or procedure. Often the people on the ground, working the machines know how best to do things, but without an understanding of the bigger picture or the desired outcome might not understand why you want or need them to be more rigid with a process – and maybe there is room for greater flexibility. You're likely to see another connection to how you communicate to figure out where and when you can be the fulcrum here.

Know Your Timeline

Even if you have a desired outcome that lends itself to greater flexibility, if you have a short time horizon, you will likely have to take a more rigid position in how you decide, plan and execute a task. In general, more resources equals greater opportunity for flexibility and nowhere is that more true than a discussion about time as a resource.

Need it done now? You probably have no room for flexibility. Got all the time in the world? Why wouldn't you want to try new techniques or methods or train your people to gain greater confidence or to take the initiative?

An understanding of your timeline is essential to understanding what the situation will allow. We'll see this again when we get to our discussion of influence.

An example from my Army experiences involves what we refer to in general terms as "targeting." Knowing your desired outcome and your timeline are the first two steps in any targeting process. If what you are trying to accomplish involves winning the hearts and minds of the local population but you need to do it in six weeks, you will take much different steps and in a more rigid fashion then you would if you knew you had six years to accomplish the same outcome.

Consider the Long-term and Immediate Impacts

Considering the long-term effects of our actions is a lot harder to do than it is to say. We live in a society that worries about the here and now: quarterly reports, twenty-four-hour news cycles, and two-year election cycles and on and on. While some cultures can think in terms of generations, most cannot. This situation is more potentially problematic for the flexible person and less so for the fixed person. If your tendency is to be flexible, you must guard against naysayers and complainers. People who are impatient will never be happy with short-term pain for long-term gain. This gets back to the importance of having a clear idea of the time it takes to achieve the desired result. If your tendency is to be fixed, you must also have a timeline in mind but before you get to the date or time when you envision the thing to be done, you must have an earlier time to begin to open up to the idea that you need to be flexible and change.

These intermediate dates will also provide structure to your adaptability component of leadership. They will serve as a forcing function to determine how effective your actions have been provided that you know what you are looking for. My recommendation in this regard is to look for the acceptable standard regardless of it being an absolute or a relative standard. Of course, I'd be crazy not to recommend that you strive for excellence in all you do, to create and lead an elite organization, but as you work your way through these issues with competing demands on your time and resources, you have to know what good enough looks like.

Perfect Can Be the Enemy

For these reasons, it's critically important that you understand the difference between sufficient and perfect. You don't need perfect information to make a decision so you shouldn't wait for perfect information to change your mind or your direction.

We have a saying in the Army that "perfect is the enemy of good." In other words, trying to make things (decisions, plans, etc.) perfect will kill you because the enemy will move faster than you can do perfect in pretty much every situation you face. Finding the balance between doing something well and doing it fast can be another way to look at it and that's why it is so important to understand what is good enough to get the job done. Of course, you want to do your best but when time is of the essence, good enough is probably the best option.

This requires you to identify measures of effectiveness or of success/failure. Once you are confident that the weight of all known evidence is sufficient to prove the success or failure of your actions, you must act. If you are by nature rigid, you must be willing to act. If you are flexible, you must trust the data and the criteria you established and stand fast when they tell you it is the right thing to do.

Politics aside, I believe that George W. Bush's decision to surge additional troops into Iraq in 2007 is a great example not only of when being rigid is the right thing to do as a leader, but also this strategy of not waiting for perfect information.

Against the counsel of nearly all his political advisors and many in the military, Bush sent an additional 20,000 troops to Baghdad and Al Anbar province and extended the tours of some units already there. The situation and information about the effectiveness of such a move was far from perfect but Bush held firm in his belief that this was the necessary step to achieve the desired outcome. It might be hard to argue cause and effect, but the fact is that following the surge, Al Qaida in Iraq was reduced significantly and the Sunni population in Al Anbar was supporting the effort to build Iraq into a stable and secure country.

You Might Be Right; You Might Be Wrong

Because we are all incredibly smart, we often only look for evidence that proves we're right once we've made a decision. This confirmation bias is troublesome at best and catastrophic at worst. It's vitally important that we not only look for proof we were right (measure of effectiveness) but also proof that we might have been wrong. It's not enough to see if things are working or not – that's a very benign view of the impact of our actions. Instead we need to realize when the plan and our actions are not working and be open to the likelihood that they are in fact making things worse. If your tendency for adaptability is rigid, you might have a real problem here. You need to open up your mind and your senses to the real possibility that you screwed things up and that you need to fix them now.

Pride might get in your way here but if you are looking to be the fulcrum with adaptability, you need to see when you are about to make a poor decision or that you did in fact make a bad decision that you should change. This too is where the domains begin to impact each other because if you are finding balance with communications and with influence at the same time, you will likely get the feedback you need to be the fulcrum with adaptability.

This doesn't mean that you don't look for confirmation of your decision making wisdom. You just need to be aware that confirmation bias is a real thing and, if you have a rigid tendency, you are more prone to its effects.

SUMMARY

- Know your tendency
- Understand what the situation demands right now: Is this a matter of principle or style?
- Know the desired outcome
- Know how much time you have to achieve that outcome
- Establish a timeline for reviewing and assessing your progress; know when you have to make a final decision to commit or change course
- Understand the difference between sufficient knowledge and perfect knowledge: Perfect is the enemy of good enough
- Look for sufficient knowledge of failure as well as success
- Move the fulcrum when you have to be flexible in the face of failure or fixed in the face of doubt

To learn more about adaptability and decision making, go to www.bethefulcrum.com and join in on the conversation. I'd love to hear your personal stories about this subject and help you become better at knowing when and how to be the fulcrum with adaptability.

FOCUS

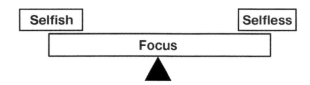

Focus

Focus: noun fo·cus \'fō-kus\

> : a subject that is being discussed or studied: the subject on which people's attention is focused

> : a **main purpose or interest**

> : a point at which rays of light, heat, or sound meet or from which they move apart or appear to move apart; especially: the point at which an image is formed by a mirror, a lens, etc.[18]

Focus Defined

Taking the definition of the word from *Merriam-Webster*, the second meaning above is the best fit for what I mean with focus as a leadership domain. What is the leader's main purpose or interest? While we could parse this many ways and say profit or mission accomplishment or reputation or legacy, it all comes down to focusing on oneself or focusing on someone

---

18. http://www.merriam-webster.com/dictionary/focus

or something else. And the nature of leadership is that one person is responsible for a group of people and an assigned task.

This is the reason I have used selfish and selfless as the opposing tendencies for focus in the Fulcrum-centric Leadership model.

Focus as a domain encompasses many aspects of what an organization or team is trying to accomplish (objective, purpose, etc.) but also how the leader and the team will get there (culture, values, etc.). And because the focus of any leadership discussion begins with the leader, I chose to define the tendencies of focus the way an individual would have to in an "either-or" or a "this versus that" framework.

It is important to remember that this model of leadership defines the tendencies of each domain in the extreme. This allows me to anchor the opposing tendencies clearly. Between the two extremes lies the place where most of us naturally fall and it's between the two extremes that the situation will demand we move to achieve balance. In some cases, that will require us to be more selfless and in other cases, it will require that we be more selfish.

Let me be clear up front, and as a departure from what I am trying to present in this book as an unbiased view of the four leadership domains, that I believe that a foundational aspect of leadership is selflessness. Next to getting the mission accomplished, taking care of their team is the most important thing a good leader does. She makes sacrifices and carries burdens too heavy for anyone else on the team. First one up, last one to sleep, whatever it takes to accomplish the task and take care of her people, the good leader will do.

One of the first lessons I learned as a brand new lieutenant was that as a leader, I got to go through the chow line only after all my men had eaten. I remember distinctly my first breakfast during field training with my platoon. It was raining as the cooks set up a row of mermites – big green buckets with lids designed to keep the food hot for the time it took to move it from the mess hall in the "rear" to the soldiers in the field. My company commander was standing there with me as soldiers filed one at a time in front of the mermites and got a spoonful each of eggs, hash browns, grits and creamed-chipped beef on toast (S.O.S as we called it) piled onto their plate. And rain. You might think that the rain made it a miserable experience but it seemed like it always rained when we were in the field. "If it ain't rainin', we ain't trainin'" was the expression that the troops used.

We had parachuted into the field the night before and then moved all night to our objective which we assaulted with blank ammunition, "killing" the enemy that held the position. Breakfast was a welcome relief, even in the rain, the common experience of most soldiers being cold, wet, tired and hungry. It was good to knock one of those down with "hot" chow, even in the rain.

Back to my company commander, and not that I was going to jump into the chow line, but he made a point of imparting wisdom on his newest lieutenant – me. "We always eat last – it's feast or famine…" An Army tradition for sure but, in the case of my boss, he was willing to bet that there would be plenty of food left and then he would pig out. Going last, the right and selfless thing to do, gave him cover to eat way more than his fair share when he could. I'm sure he went last also because going first would really have exposed him as being selfish. I never really liked that guy for a lot of reasons but his hypocrisy that morning in the woods of Fort Bragg planted a seed in my mind that grew to become this chapter of this book.

Simon Sinek used that military tradition for the title of his book Leaders Eat Last. From the title alone, you might think that his book is about selfless service but it's really about creating an environment where everyone on the team can feel good about what they are doing and also accomplish great things. Ultimately Sinek promotes the idea (and it's a great idea) that leaders should look to take care of their people as a way for the organization to thrive. The concept of "Servant Leader"[19] does this as well and I can get behind both these concepts but, in my opinion, they miss one big point.

In any endeavor, not just the military, being selfless is a virtue. It is high-lighted in the military because of the risks and sacrifices inherent in the job. But I have seen leaders fail, personally and professionally, more often than not because they could not find the balance between what they wanted (selfish) and what the organization expected of them (selfless). And that's the big point: to be successful, the leader must find balance between their tendency for focus and what the situation demands, even if that means going for their self-interest in that moment.

While it's fairly easy to find people writing or talking about the role and duty of the leader to be selfless, it's much harder to find folks who will

---

19. From Wikipedia: "Unlike leadership approaches with a top-down hierarchical style, servant leadership instead emphasizes collaboration, trust, empathy, and the ethical use of power. At heart, the individual is a servant first, making the conscious decision to lead in order to better serve others, not to increase their own power." https://en.wikipedia.org/wiki/Servant_leadership

praise selfish as a virtue. It seems as a culture we value selflessness above all else with the possible exception being "trust." This is certainly my experience in military cultures. Much has been written about the vice of selfishness but very little about when and how there is any virtue in being selfish. There are some exceptions to this generalization; Ayn Rand (author of *Atlas Shrugged* and *The Fountainhead*), Gene Simmons (bassist for KISS and author of *ME Inc.*) and James Altucher (author of *Choose Yourself*) come to mind but you really need to dig to find people who talk about any goodness in looking out for one's own best interests. This is clearly the most difficult domain to balance perhaps because we view the two tendencies so differently; Selfless = Good, Selfish = Bad. But when we judge a leader or a person to be selfish or selfless, what are we really judging? It's a person's behaviors that lead us to judge their motives but can we truly know what is deeply motivating people? This is one of the dark secrets of leadership and one that we all wrestle with but few among us will admit it when we act purely in our own self-interest. We often frame it as "doing it for the good of the team" or "stepping up to the challenge." Both these cases may in fact have some measure of selfless service or altruism in their origins but let's be honest that self-interest can be the driving force for a lot of the things we do.

And here is another truth: Selfish is about what you won't do as much as it is about what you will do. Not taking on a challenge or not accepting a role with greater responsibility can be just as selfish as making sure you are recognized for your efforts or doing whatever it takes to win that promotion. Outwardly, these are two drastically different outcomes but inwardly, the reason for each is the same: individual desire over group. So, an act cannot be truly assessed as selfish or selfless without knowing the motivation of the actor.

What really matters is how you focus for a particular situation. We can talk all day about the virtues of selflessness but there are certain situations where selfishness is required and that's a fact. Don't believe me? Then I bet you've never flown on a plane.

I travel a lot and when I do, I usually fly Delta Airlines. I've flown others so I know that Delta isn't the only airline to engage in this practice but every time I fly, Delta asks me and every other person on the plane to do something selfish should the situation arise. Think about it and you'll know exactly what I'm talking about. Just before takeoff on every flight, there is a safety briefing given by the flight attendants.

"Should we experience a sudden loss of cabin pressure; oxygen masks will fall from the overhead compartments…"

Now you know what I'm talking about. After the instructions on how to put that yellow cup over your nose and mouth, comes this request to be selfish:

"If you are traveling with a child or someone who requires assistance, secure your mask first and then assist the other person."

It doesn't matter what your natural tendency is for focus, the moment that those oxygen masks fall from above you, the situation demands that you engage in a selfish act. It doesn't matter that it only takes a few seconds to put on the mask in the safety demonstration; there's a very good reason for you to be selfish. If you've ever been in an airplane that loses pressure and is falling quickly or in heavy turbulence, you know that it will likely take you more than a few seconds to secure that mask and get it over your nose and mouth. If you didn't secure your mask first, you and the child or person needing assistance might become incapacitated.

Albeit a brief situation and one that rarely happens, the airline safety briefing is the perfect example of a situation dictating you to do something different from your tendency--assuming that you fall somewhere on the selfless side of the domain. In doing it, you become the fulcrum and balance is restored. In a more deliberate and intentional situation, you might have to do more to assess the situation but if you know your natural tendency going in, it will be easier to see what direction you need to move to effectively rebalance the situation.

More than any of the other domains discussed in this book, focus demands honesty in knowing our tendency and clarity in when, why and how we become the fulcrum. Focus is also a trait that matters most in the long-term to achieve balance; you may find yourself in a situation where a selfish act now and in this situation will lead to mission accomplishment and greater good for the team. On a larger scale, I would call this the need to "do well now so I can do good later." An example of this might be your drive to make millions of dollars now but to spend most of that money in the future to help others when you establish your philanthropic foundation. Whatever their motivation to build Microsoft and the billions that they are worth, Bill and Melinda Gates would not be able to do all the good they are doing now if they had not done so well in their prime earning years.

It's likely that we all have our selfish moments and that even when we are doing something selfless, there is some reward or a positive return on our investment. I'm okay with that and you should be too. The key is in understanding why it might be best to act selfish and being totally honest with ourselves.

Motivation, innovation and progress are often the child of someone's selfish desires. Yet selfish as a tendency is a pariah and while it may be a cultural thing to "hate" it, there no doubt is good that can come of it. I will also bet that of the four domains, most of us are more self-aware of our tendency for focus.

Here is another interesting thing about focus; we think, see and attribute the tendencies in others more easily than we recognize or admit them in ourselves.

Think about the last time you made a choice that had an impact on someone or something bigger than yourself. What drove you to make that choice? Was it to gain some benefit for yourself or was it something for that larger group? Did you truly have to give anything up in making that choice or was it a relatively painless choice?

Sometimes we do things that are selfless but only because they are also easy or obviously the right thing to do. The real measure of selflessness is sacrifice; what do you give up in return for your altruism? In many cases, only you can answer that question and in many cases, it matters little. But we have placed so much value on selflessness that selfishness gets a bad rap.

You may have seen the Cadillac commercial with Steve Wozniak (co-founder of Apple Computer) lying on a couch, headphones on, very expensive record turntable in the foreground. He says that he didn't make the Apple Computer because he was selfish; he did it because he wanted to give free computers to the world. I see it a little differently. Here's a transcript of the voice over from that commercial:

> "...its effects on society really came about because, not because I was selfish and wanted one for myself, which I did, it's because I had had a passion my whole life. I wanted to teach myself to build computers. I wanted to build these things for free; I just wanted to do it for the world. And, you know, when you want something, that's what you do the best."

Because he doesn't say it explicitly in this voice over, I can only assume that the thing having an "effect on society" Wozniak is talking about is the personal computer. Arguably, people around the world have lived better, richer lives because of the products that Apple makes. And Steve Wozniak seems to be a generous man by all accounts but if we could go back forty plus years and ask the young Steve Wozniak why he was doing this, what he hoped to achieve, I imagine that the selfishness of it all might come out a bit more if he were being totally honest. He admits as much at the end – "...when you want something, that's what you do the best."

I'm not suggesting that the ends justify the means; what I am suggesting is that some amount of selfishness can be a good thing. That it drives us to do bigger and better, even greater things. Understand how strong a tendency it is for you and use it when the situation dictates. If you are a naturally selfless individual, recognize that sometimes you have to be selfish in order to move yourself or your team forward. In Wozniak's case, I truly believe, whether he knew it or not or can admit it or not, what he did with Apple was "doing well to do good."

While doing research for this chapter, I came across a story by Daniel Goleman that had been excerpted from his book *A Force for Good*. The story is an account of a conversation he had with the Dalai Lama wherein the Lama talked about the value of good will and love to all, including the person giving the love. The Dalai Lama used the terms "wise selfish" and "foolish selfish" to describe things we do for ourselves that have value versus things we do for ourselves only for ourselves. Sounds a lot like how most of us would differentiate between selfless and selfish but I like the Dalai Lama's thinking on this:

"It is important that when pursing our own self-interest we should be 'wise selfish' and not 'foolish selfish.'" Being foolish selfish means pursuing our own interests in a narrow, shortsighted way. Being wise selfish means taking a broader view and recognizing that our own long-term individual interest lies in the welfare of everyone. Being wise selfish means being compassionate."[20]

The Bigger Picture and Selfishness versus Selflessness

Towards the end of my military career, I was fortunate enough to be a part of a Special Operations Task Force and to serve with the most amazing men and women in uniform. Judiciously selected among their

---

20. http://jasminbalance.com/quote-we-should-be-wise-selfish-and-not-foolish-selfish/

peers as the best at what they did, this was (and is) the "Dream Team" of military organizations.

I returned to Afghanistan in the fall of 2003 with the task force, having spent the first seven months of that year in country with my battalion. One of the main reasons I was sent back to Afghanistan was that there were some points of friction, minor misunderstandings really, between the conventional forces in Afghanistan and what was at the time a largely Navy staffed Special Operations Task Force. My job was to help the two sides better understand each other but mostly to protect the equities of the task force.

At about the same time that I was sent back to Afghanistan, there was a "bin Laden sighting" and so the task force, which was beginning the fight against Al Qaeda in Iraq (AQI) surged back into Afghanistan in search of the top target. As we now know, bin Laden wasn't in Afghanistan but in Pakistan where the task force eventually found and killed him on May 2nd 2011 in Abbottabad. But before that fateful night raid, we were tracking down bin Laden and his followers on the Afghan side of that very poorly defined border between Afghanistan and Pakistan.

At some point in the late fall of 2003, this particular surge was called off but I remained in Afghanistan with the task force and served briefly as the operations officer. Our mission was to continue to take the fight to Al Qaeda in Afghanistan but to be ready and able to "Find, Fix and Finish" senior Al Qaeda leadership no matter where they were in the Afghanistan-Pakistan (AF-PAK) region.

Between the conventional forces and the task force in country, we had some fairly well established bases in the northeastern parts of Afghanistan (Jalalabad and Khost) and at the two main facilities at that time (Bagram and Kandahar) but only small bases in other parts of the country. There was only one small base in southeast Afghanistan at a place called Shkin and it was under near constant attack from indirect fire and ambush parties from across the nearby border.

The conventional forces under the command of then Major General Lloyd Austin decided to follow through with a plan that his predecessor in Afghanistan, Lieutenant General John Vines, had put in motion – close the base at Shkin. At the same time, the intelligence community was of a mind that they could run the majority of their operations out of Kabul and that they would leave southeastern Afghanistan when the base at Shkin was shuttered.

All that started to happen around the New Year, and the effect was immediate; the Taliban claimed a victory in driving us out of Shkin.

I knew that we had to do something, and that if we ever needed to operate in southeastern Afghanistan, or even across the border in South Waziristan, Pakistan, we needed a base to stage from. I pulled my team together and tasked them to look for alternative base locations with the criteria that it had to allow for the construction of a runway for resupply. Helicopters were at a premium and travel by road was difficult and becoming more dangerous with IEDs. I wanted a base that could support a minimum of a short takeoff and landing (STOL) aircraft but ideally a C-130.[21]

We looked at the alternatives that the conventional forces had considered and searched for some new locations of our own. What we found was an open plateau along a route running from Pakistan into Afghanistan. What we built there was a large base with a C-17 capable runway, much greater capability than I ever envisioned. But the selling point to constructing this new base wasn't that it would be a good replacement for the lost base at Shkin but that it would send a message to the Pakistani authorities: "Fix the problems on your side of the border or we'll come over to fix them for you."

It wasn't until my final briefing to the admiral in charge of the task force that this even occurred to me but it was in fact the best reason to do this. The proof is in the increased levels of activity that the Pakistan military conducted in the "Tribal Areas" once we started to build our new airfield. In South Waziristan alone, the Pakistan military presence increased seven-fold.

You might wonder at this point, how is this related to focus? Good question.

Bill McRaven could have been selfless and played along with the plans and desires of the conventional forces in Afghanistan; he could have been a "team player." But the Special Operations Task Force had a very specific mission to accomplish and tools and resources at its command that other organizations did not have. Building that airfield required the tasking of an engineer battalion out of Fort Bragg. I'm not sure where or when that battalion would have been employed if not used to build FOB Carlson but I know from talking with the men of that unit that building that base and runway was a dream come true.

---

21. The Air Force designates aircraft based on their function; bombers are B's (B-1, B-2, etc.); fighters are F's (F-16, F-22, etc.) and cargo aircraft are C's (C-130, C17, etc.). A C-130 has four turbo-prop engines and can land easily on dirt or grass runways. A C-17 is has four jet engines and requires a longer, harder surface for landings and take-offs.

By being a little selfish, McRaven and the task force were able to drive events and leverage other resources for the better. Had we not built FOB Carlson, there is no telling how much more trouble we would have seen coming from the Pakistan side of the border. By making a decision that was in the best interest of his command, Admiral McRaven achieved goodness in the fight against Al Qaeda.

I'd add too that he might have been putting himself at risk with the senior officers in Afghanistan or in the military hierarchy at Central Command. It seems to me that it didn't matter to McRaven. He was doing what he thought was right. That made this a matter of principle so he stood his ground and we built a base that might have pissed off other general officers.

My point here is that organizationally, his actions could be seen as selfish but personally, and because he was potentially taking a risk, Admiral McRaven was also being selfless. Clearly, it didn't hurt him and Bill McRaven went on to earn a fourth star and command of all Special Operations.

I've never asked McRaven what his motivation was so I'd be assuming if I wrote about it here. But I was the other key player in this plan and I can tell you honestly that my reason for putting the idea of this base forward was in part due to a selfish desire to prove I could do something of value with this organization.

This was different from anything else I had done before and it had the potential (I knew) to impact the war without firing a shot or killing anyone. But beyond the value and the long-term impact of this action, at that moment, I had a chance to prove wrong the three-star general who said to me, "you don't have anything to offer the task force" when I left command of my battalion six months earlier.

Had it gone poorly, my selfishness would certainly have been to blame and in retrospect, it would have been justly deserved for someone to assign that to me. But the same could be true for selfless acts – it is only in retrospect when we can say if that selfless act had a "good" or a "bad" effect. Why not the same of selfishness?

Self-Awareness

So, where does that leave you, the leader of your organization or team?

As with the other domains, you must assess your natural tendency first. This one will be harder to do than the other three because of the way we look at and judge anything labeled "selfish." You'll have to guard against that bias and honestly look at yourself and how you behave in different situations. In general, however:

You Have a Tendency to Be Selfish If:

- Your first thought is always "what's in this for me?"
- When something goes wrong, you look to justify/prove it wasn't your fault
- You are true to your personal wants and desires
- You are not willing to make a sacrifice (right now)
- Your criteria for making a decision always involves personal costs, sacrifice or pain

You Have a Tendency to Be Selfless If:

- Your first thought is always "what's best for the team?"
- When something goes wrong, you accept full responsibility no matter the consequences
- You put other's needs first
- You are willing to make any sacrifice (right now)
- Your criteria for making a decision never involves personal costs, sacrifice or pain

If you make every decision with a calculation of "What's in this for me?" you are being selfish. That could be the end of the discussion right there but we need to dig a little deeper because this is not always or not necessarily a bad thing.

If "what's in this for me?" is ALWAYS your first thought, then you are most definitely selfish and probably not in any way that is good. If, however, that comes into consideration later, you are still displaying selfish tendencies but in a calculated manner. Your time, efforts and resources are a precious thing and you have to use them wisely. If you cannot consider what the impact of a choice or decision is on you and your future – your ability to continue to do good things – then you will ultimately fail to achieve your greatest potential and your greatest satisfaction.

We need to be honest when talking about selfless tendencies and admit that for some of us, it's much easier to be selfless when things are going well; a much harder thing is to be selfless when things are going badly.

I believe that true selflessness involves sacrifice, which usually means pain. What pain are you willing to endure? If you are not willing to take the blame when things go wrong with your team, are you displaying a selfish tendency? The issue then comes down to what is justly your blame or your pain to take on. You might want to accept responsibility for something that has gone wrong and thereby protect your team, your peers or even your boss from some sort of pain or problem. If you were at fault, that's not really selflessness; that's honesty and accountability. If it wasn't your fault, it might look like a selfless act to take the blame, but if, for example, you were looking for an easy way out of a bad situation, you might take the fall to save yourself from having to make the difficult decision to leave. In that case, I would argue that you were being totally selfish.

We all have desires and things that we want. Even something as noble and far-reaching as "world peace" begins with a personal desire and that, by measure, makes it somewhat selfish. This fact gives credence to the idea that selfish/selfless is a function of our judgment or perception of the outcome. If I selfishly want world peace and steadfastly do only those things I think will accomplish it, am I not selfish? The answer to that question is probably influenced by my actions and my attitudes as well. If you are an ass about your selfish desires, even world peace, you can successfully achieve that goal – but still be an ass. In this case, it will likely be easier for the rest of us to recognize your selfish tendency.

One of the things that makes us seem selfish or selfless is how we interact with people in the process and how we share the fruits of our labors. More on that to follow but if you can bring more people into your personal vision and desires, if you can share the process and the outcomes with as many people as possible, then good deeds will be seen as selfless no matter the origins of your motivation. I think this is what the Dalai Lama meant by "wise selfish."

The flip side of that coin is that if you share (inflict) process and outcomes for bad things, your deeds will be seen as selfish. There is a saying:

"We judge others by their behaviors but we judge ourselves by our good intentions."[22] Bottom line: don't let your intentions or other's deeds mislead you as to what is selfish and what is selfless.

While it is easy to assign a negative quality to selfishness and a positive quality to selflessness, there are times and situations where selfish is the positive and selfless is the negative tendency to exhibit.

Situational Awareness

Sometimes people will use the superior nature of selfless to shame us into doing things for them. "Take one for the team" or "You need to be a team player" are two expressions I heard way too much in the Army. In my experience, it was usually a peer or a senior officer trying to disguise their selfish tendencies behind a claim or a demand that I or someone else needed to be selfless. I remember a peer battalion commander who in July of 2001 wanted to take the entire brigade's annual allocation of ammunition so that he and his battalion could test a new marksmanship training program. The selling point was that he would be able to validate the effectiveness of this new program and we would all be better for it in the long run. The price, however, was that my battalion and the other battalion in our brigade would not be able to do any live-fire training that year; we were being asked to be "team players." I'd like to think that my tendency is to be more selfless than selfish but I had to resist it here and tell my fellow battalion commander no ("no" is not exactly what I told him, but my editor told me we couldn't print what I actually said).

As it turned out, the summer of 2001 was not the time to be selfless with ammunition. After 9/11 we needed all that we could get our hands on to train our soldiers for the coming combat mission in Afghanistan. My point here is that selflessness is often about context; who benefits from the act and is there a difference between immediate and long-term effect?

True selflessness is often an instinctive act with real sacrifice attached to it. The soldier who falls on a grenade to shield his fellow soldiers from harm is an obvious example. This is another thing that makes the shift between selfless and selfish so hard to do; it requires a deliberate decision to do one or the other. I would submit that selfishness, in this case self-preservation, is instinctive while selflessness is driven more by culture. In this light, and especially with regards to leadership, focus becomes a nature versus nurture issue.

---

22. Not sure of the exact origins of this quotation but most attribute it to Steven Covey or Ian Percy.

Like Steve Wozniak, I believe that pursuing what you want, and what you are good at, is better for everyone in the long run. I also believe that selflessness is a noble and wonderful thing.

But the point of this book and the main idea of Fulcrum-centric Leadership is that the situation that we are leading in demands what we need to do as a leader. The problem for most of us comes when the situations demands we do something opposite or different in some degree from our natural tendency. Maybe it would be better to say our preferred tendency but with focus there is another thing going on that is not so powerful in the other three domains. Our cultural bias against selfishness makes it harder to be the fulcrum in this domain when the situation demands it.

For all the reasons I've already stated, this is the hardest domain to understand and the hardest to do. Just admitting our natural tendency can be difficult, especially when all the indicators put us on the side of selfish. Then the equally hard task of assessing the situation comes into play. It's hardly ever as obvious as yellow oxygen masks appearing right in front of your eyes...

Who Is the Best Person or Team to Do This?

In any situation, there is usually someone who is best suited to do the work. Even when skill or knowledge seems even, other factors will likely come into play when we consider the outcome and our time horizon. It's not a coincidence that these factor into the situation when we consider being the fulcrum with adaptability and influence as well but with focus they play a critical role.

If you can honestly and openly admit that some other person or some other team within your company is better suited to do the task, even if it's something you really want to do, then the situation dictates selflessness.

On the other hand, if you or your team is the best suited to do a task, then focus shouldn't matter. But what if you don't want to do this thing? What if you have some competing requirement for your time and efforts? What if the other thing that you want to do will be better for everyone (you included) in the long run? Is it selfish for you to do the one you want to do over the one that you are the best at doing?

Perhaps a cost-benefit analysis is the only thing you can do to resolve this problem. I'm not a big fan of numbers but I am a fan of analysis and vision. If you can see where you can have the greatest good for the greatest number of people for the longest time, then you should be selfish or selfless to that end.

Ultimately, we must be willing to assess ourselves and our teams and step up when the answer to this question is "me/us" or step aside when the answer is "you/them."

What Are We/I Really Trying to Accomplish?

Another way to gauge the situation to see where you should hold your focus is to understand what you are really trying to accomplish. If your goal is to achieve a task in the quickest amount of time possible, then you might selfishly take on that task. But if you are trying to develop your team or help out a colleague, perhaps it makes more sense to be selfless and give up the opportunity to someone else. The task at hand gets accomplished but so does the real task of training and developing the team. This is where the mantra of "do well, then do good" can take on powerful meaning.

If what you are trying to accomplish is a world where personal computers are affordable, if not free, then selfishly pursuing your desire to build a company like Apple is what the situation demands. Think of all the people who have found work building Apple products; think of all the people who have become more connected with the world because of Apple products. Apple products aren't known for being inexpensive but they are known for quality and they certainly have had an impact on other products available in the market. Would there be a market for a $300 laptop if Apple wasn't making $3000 laptops?

Bill Gates of Microsoft might even be a better example. When he dropped out of Harvard to pursue his desire to start a computer software company, he was acting selfishly but that's really what his situation dictated. He was doing what he was good at or as Joseph Campbell would say, he was following his bliss. I'm not sure what selfless would have looked like in that situation and you can debate whether or not Microsoft is a good company but there is no denying that the Bill and Melinda Gates Foundation has done great charitable work.

Only Gates can tell us if giving away billions of dollars in donations and grants was what he was really trying to accomplish when he set out to build Microsoft but my guess is that the idea was there someplace. There is no telling if he would have been able to accomplish the same thing if he had stayed at Harvard until graduation but I'm guessing that his family wanted him to stay in school and may not have viewed that as selfless; they probably called him selfish when he dropped out.

What Is Being Incentivized?

Another way to assess your situation is to look at the incentives in the environment: which actions or outcomes are being incentivized and which are being penalized?

If you find yourself in a situation where people are acting selfishly but you want or need them to be more selfless, it's likely that something is working as an incentive to be selfish. The opposite is equally true but rarely seen. Still it is possible that people are not properly motivated to act in their best interests even when they should be.

I'll go back to my military career for an example here. The path to command and promotion for an Infantry officer like me has always been assignments with combat units. Take an assignment "away from troops" and you are putting your career and your chances for higher level command at risk. The Army needs good people in all types of assignments, especially in its schools, yet the promotion and selection systems seem to work as an incentive to keep the best out of the classroom. Until the Army figures out a way to reward with promotions and commands the people who serve outside of tactical units, it will have a hard time getting its best and most talented officers and NCO's to teach the next generation of soldiers. Don't get me wrong, there are some fine officers and NCO's who leave the operational Army for the institutional Army and do well, but all will probably agree that they are putting their career at risk.

But here is the paradox of this situation: The Army needs good people in the classroom, but soldiers who take that path are often looked at as "quitters" or as taking a break from the really important job of being in a deployable unit. Those soldiers are called selfish by some, even though it's probably more appropriate to say they are being selfless, putting their career at risk for the good of the next generation of soldiers and the future of the Army.

Action versus Inaction

Selfishness doesn't always show up as someone doing something in their own self-interest; it can also show up as inaction – doing nothing when something is needed. The extreme example of this is the person who does nothing during an assault on a stranger in a public place. Fight, flight and freeze are the three instinctive responses to danger. Stepping in to help seems selfless; running away seems selfish; freezing is a selfish focus too. These are generalities and we'd need to know more to make an accurate assessment. For instance, is the person stepping in looking for an excuse to fight or hurt someone? Then it becomes less selfless and more selfish. What if the person running away is risking hazards to go find help? That seems less selfish and more selfless.

Inaction or freezing can be considered the same way as fight or flight. We have to understand the action in context and with some idea of the actor's intentions.

My point in all of this is that you have to see what your people will not do and why to understand if the situation demands a shift in focus.

Strategies for Being the Fulcrum with Focus

- Ask the question: "If not me, then who?"

- Understand what you really want to achieve and why

- Identify both the long-term and short-term impacts of your action or your decision

- First seek to do well. Then seek to do good

Ask the Best Question

In becoming the fulcrum for focus, the first question you must ask and answer of yourself is this: "If not me, then who?" The beauty of this question is that it can move you in either direction on the lever of focus and, in either case, it might cause you to step up or step aside.

When the situation dictates a more selfish focus, you will know it in your answer if you are the best person to do a task or take on a position. If you have other priorities and there is someone else to do this task in question, a selfish focus will let you know it's okay not to take on this new duty – someone else can and will get it done.

When the situation dictates a more selfless focus, your answer to the question will be that someone else or some other team is better suited to do it. You might have to swallow your pride but if you have a good assessment of the situation, it will be the right thing to do. If, on the other hand, there is no one else to do this task, and even if you have a full calendar or task list, being selfless and taking on this extra load is probably the right thing to do.

You will have an easier time answering that question if you can set aside for the moment the thought of any rewards or pain that might come with the action. There will be a time and a place for that later when you look to assess the impact in the long and short run. For now, you just need to assess who is the best person to do the thing that needs to be done (task, mission, job or position all fall into this general category of "thing"). Objectively, without concern for the sacrifice or for the glory, when you can answer "if not me, then who?" you can see where your talents are needed most. It doesn't matter at this point if that is a selfish or selfless move; what matters is that you see your place and your role accurately.

What Is Your Motivation?

The next step in being the fulcrum for focus is to understand what you really want to achieve and why you want to achieve it. What we're talking about here is a personal goal and vision statement. You don't need to wait for a situation where you have to be the fulcrum to do this; in fact, it's probably too late if you find yourself in this situation and don't already know.

During my time working at the Army Center for Enhanced Performance at Fort Bragg, I saw the importance of goal setting and attainment with the soldiers whom we helped. I saw it but I didn't take the time to objectively evaluate for myself that personal vision. That's probably why it's taken me so long to write this book – over ten years – because I didn't write down what I wanted to achieve with it and why. Knowing what you want is okay but writing it down makes it tangible.

James Kerr in his book *Legacy* writes about New Zealand's All Blacks captain, Richie McCaw, setting goals to be a Great All Black with the help of his uncle Bugsy. "If it isn't written, it isn't real," his uncle tells him. Sage advice and such a simple act with such a lasting impact.

For me, the realization of the importance for understanding what I wanted and why came as I took on a personal coach to help me write this book. But in digging deeper for my goals and purpose, she helped me see the bigger picture and the purpose I bring with me. I believe strongly in Fulcrum-centric Leadership but it's a perspective that I've not seen articulated in the same way by anyone else. So, I had to ask myself, "If not me, then who?" And I had to understand and know my intentions and purpose in writing this book. My coach helps me stay accountable to my goals and my vision but they are my goals and my purpose. And they are more real now because I took the time to write them down.

So, these are the first two steps: the answer to the "if not me, then who?" question and knowing what you want to achieve and why. They allow you to be selfless or selfish as the situation demands because they force you to be honest about your motivation and to assess if there is anyone else who can or should do the job. Knowing your natural tendency before you get to this point is vitally important because you are likely to see and feel resistance in this domain when you have to be the fulcrum and move away from that preferred tendency.

Imagine the Future

Another way to help you know when and how to be the fulcrum in focus is to see the short- and long-term effects of your actions and decisions. What might seem to only benefit you in moving the fulcrum to selfish in the short-term could actually be the best thing for your company in the long-term. We can say the same when we move towards selflessness and a short-term positive becomes a long-term negative.

Understanding the impact of your actions as a leader, not just guessing at them but making the effort to see the second and third level effects as well as the immediate effect, will help you to be the fulcrum as you need to be.

If I seem to talk mostly about when, why and how to be selfish, it's only because we rarely talk about it as an option for a leader. It's there and it is a viable choice when we need to direct our focus as leaders, no matter how culturally distasteful it is to be selfish. I've seen leaders who wrap themselves in the cloak of selflessness only to hide their true intentions. I'd rather they be honest about what they are doing and why they are doing it so long as they can communicate the value in their actions.

If you are trying to move your team one way or the other with focus, personal example and explanations are your watch words. Your people are watching your every move. Set the example you need them to follow and explain why you are doing this – communications and influence in action.

Ultimately, leadership is about service and giving back to others, which sounds an awful lot like selflessness. It's no wonder then that one of the

---

23. The Army values are: Loyalty, Duty, Respect, Selfless Service, Honor, Integrity and Personal Courage. As a pneumonic, they spell LDRSHIP, which sounds like leadership.

core values of the United States Army is "selfless service."[23] But focus as a domain is really about intentions; if it's possible for someone to do something that seems selfless but with selfish intentions, was it a selfless or a selfish act? Same thing applies when we go the other way, a selfish act but with selfless intentions.

Both scenarios are possible and both selfless and selfish can move an organization forward. The key for us in the final analysis – and it goes back to our culture – is this: Is there some good that comes out of the action?

Remember what I said at the very beginning of this book. The situation is dynamic and constantly changing. If you as a leader find yourself in a situation that demands a selfish focus, you must be selfish or you might fail. Like the yellow oxygen masks that fall from the ceiling of the airplane, these situations are possible and they usually require short-term action for long-term positive effect. Don't discount the reality of selfish just because we are talking about leadership. You cannot be a good leader and be selfish for long but chances are you won't be a leader much longer if you pass on a chance to do something important just because you thought it was selfish.

SUMMARY

- Know your tendency
- Understand what the situation demands right now: a selfless act or looking out for yourself?
- Can or will anyone else do this? Is there someone better suited to take the task?
- What is the immediate impact of this action? What is the more lasting effect?
- If you want to do good in the world, it helps to do well first

INFLUENCE

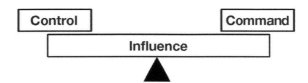

Influence

Influence: noun: in·flu·ence \'in-flü-en(t)s, especially Southern in-'\

: the power to change or affect someone or something: the power to cause changes without directly forcing them to happen

: a person or thing that affects someone or something in an important way[24]

Influence Defined

Command and control (or C2 in military parlance) has long been a tenet of military operations but the term has been replaced recently with the phrase "mission command." This change in terminology is designed primarily to stress the need for initiative in junior leaders and subordinate units but it also reflects the role of the leader to empower through the allocation of resources and a clear statement of intent. Mission command is often held up as a contrast or as something different than what is often called a command and control method or style of leadership. In many leadership

---

24. http://www.merriam-webster.com/dictionary/influence

books, the term command and control is used to describe a more directive style of leadership, on the low or less evolved end of scale.

In the book *Primal Leadership*, Daniel Goleman and his co-authors list "command and control" at the very bottom of their leadership styles model; it is one of two "dissonant" styles of leadership.[25]

While I can understand that "command and control" can be used as a descriptive for a style of leadership, it is incorrect and unfair to suggest that it is the cause of dissonance in a group or with the followers in an organization. I believe that the cause of dissonance in any organization is conflict and a lack of balance. It's perhaps my familiarity with the terms, and I'll explain how I see them below, but when taken as the opposite tendencies of influence, command and control are the best markers for the extremes in this domain.

My perspective is that the term should have always been command versus control because both serve an important function and both have their proper place in leadership and in leading organizations. The trick and the real skill comes with, you guessed it, finding the right balance between the two for any given situation.

Let's begin this discussion by defining the terms in the way I see them and how they work with and against each other.

Command is art. It is the art of influence and influence is the essence of leadership. Command is an indirect way to achieve results and is practiced through ideas and intention. Command is inclusive because it allows – no, it demands – initiative and engagement from subordinates. The operative word with command is "why."

Control is science. It is the science of direction and action which are essential to outcomes. Control is a direct way to achieve results and is practiced through specific instruction and oversight. The operative word with control is "how."

Just like the other three domains, there are times and places when it's more appropriate to control than to command and vice-versa. Again, the key is to begin with an understanding of your natural tendency and then check it against the situation.

---

25. Goleman, Daniel et al, "Primal Leadership: Unleashing the Power of Emotional Intelligence." For Goleman, leadership styles all have their appropriate place but there is a clear hierarchy moving from "command and control" at the far end of dissonance to "visionary" at the far end of resonance

Know How + Know Why = No How

In November of 1988, not yet twenty-eight years old, I assumed command of the Anti-Armor Company in the 2nd Battalion of the 325th Airborne Infantry Regiment (D/2-325 AIR). I was originally scheduled to command one of the rifle companies in the battalion; that would have been a dream come true and the goal of every infantry captain who serves in the 82nd Airborne Division. The change from "Bravo" Company to "Delta" Company was due to the battalion's poor performance in an external evaluation ("EXEVAL" for short) that happened soon after I arrived to the battalion. An EXEVAL is a tactical exercise that attempts to simulate combat for the purpose of assessing a unit's combat readiness. The last two missions the battalion had to execute were total disasters due to Delta Company screwing things up – actually, it was the company commander who screwed things up. Delta Company was a wreck and the morning after the battalion came in from the field, the battalion commander called me into his office.

"Mike, I know we said that you would command Bravo Company but Delta Company is broken and I think you are the guy to fix it." I thanked him for his confidence and let him know that I would do my best – "Put me in coach" was what came out of my mouth but on the inside I was mad as hell.

I had previously commanded the Long Range Surveillance Troop (LRST) in the Air Cavalry Squadron of the 82nd Airborne Division (D/1-17 CAV). This was the most elite company in the 82nd; our mission was to go in early before an airborne operation to report on enemy activity or to go behind enemy lines to watch for and report on high value targets. All of my soldiers were Ranger qualified and many came to us from the Ranger Regiment. One soldier, whom I brought with me from my old unit when I took command of the LRST, would go on in about twenty years to become the Command Sergeant Major of an elite Special Operations unit. It was a very specialized Airborne Ranger unit with a very special mission using the best people we could find.

While a rifle company was a step down from the LRST in terms of eliteness, an Anti-Armor Company was considered even more so – they rode on HMMWVs. And because they rode instead of walked, they were considered "soft" by most of their peers. It was such a pervasive attitude that most of the infantry officers without a Ranger Tab were sent to the Delta Company in their battalion.

Changing that culture within our company and within the battalion was one of my long-term objectives but first I had to make sure that D/2-325 was an effective fighting force. While is seems like an obvious change to make in most organizations that are ineffective, changing the structure is often the last thing you should do. In the case of the Anti-Armor Companies of the 82nd, it was the first thing needing to be done.

When I took command, the standard in the 82nd was that all nine Anti-Armor Companies were organized exactly the same: Five platoons of six vehicles (four "gun trucks," one command vehicle for the platoon leader and one cargo HMMWV for the platoon sergeant). Of the five platoons, two were primarily equipped with the M2 .50 Cal heavy machine gun while the other three platoons were primarily equipped with the TOW[26] Anti-Tank missile system.

This configuration was ineffective and in my mind totally unsuited to what the battalion really needed in the only company it had that was 100% motorized and had the majority of the firepower.[27] In short, here was the problem: the configuration was a totally defensive orientation. One of the 82nd Airborne's key tasks at the time was something called the Airborne Anti-Armor Defense or "Triple-A D" for short. TOW platoons in this configuration would be primarily static to take on the waves of Soviet tanks and armored vehicles while the .50 Cal platoons covered "dismounted" avenues of approach. While this might work against the Soviet hoards, it was a poor use of assets in most other scenarios.

I felt that we needed an offensive capability and with it an offensive mindset. I needed our soldiers to dismount their vehicles while doing reconnaissance or screening missions. I felt that in an urban environment, we needed to know how to move and position our vehicles but also how to enter and clear buildings. These were not tasks that were recognized by the division or by the Army for my company but my experience up to that point told me otherwise.

---

26. TOW: It is an acronym for "Tube-launched, Optically-tracked, Wire guided." At the time, this was the most sophisticated and accurate anti-armor weapon system in the world. It had a range of 3.75 KM but the gunner needed to track his target from launch to missile impact making the crew vulnerable to enemy fire for the entire flight time, requiring AT crews to have spines of steel and balls of brass. The current version of this weapon system is wireless but you still have to track the target until the missile impacts.

27. At the time, the 82nd Airborne Division comprised three infantry brigades, an artillery brigade, an aviation brigade and seven "separate" battalions for other functions (armor, military intelligence, engineers, signal, logistics, maintenance and medical). Each of the infantry brigades had three battalions and each battalion had five companies (three rifle companies, one Anti-Armor Company and one headquarters company).

Commanding the LRST was a great experience and I learned a lot from it but even more important for my time commanding Delta Company was the year I spent in 1-17 CAV after giving up command of the LRST, serving as the squadron intelligence officer. Back then it was rare for an infantry officer to serve in an aviation unit or a cavalry unit and here I was doing both. Even rarer still was the chance to work as an intelligence officer. I learned as much in that one year as I did in the four previous combined. One of the best things about it was that I got the chance to watch and observe one of the other troops in the cavalry squadron, the Ground Cav Troop (A/1-17 CAV). The ground cavalry was a company sized unit with TOW systems and .50 Cal machine guns, just like the Anti-Armor Companies of the infantry battalions but their mission was to find, fix and, where possible, finish the enemy. Each platoon of the ground cavalry troop had a mix of both TOW and .50 Cal, not separate platoons of each. They were organized to dismount their vehicles too so that they could extend their capability to more restrictive terrain. This became my model but it was more than just a structural change; it was a change in mission and a change in thinking and both would require that my men were willing and able to perform in this manner.

With five platoons of six vehicles, the assigned number of soldiers in each vehicle of Delta Company was three each on the "gun" trucks and two each on the command and support vehicles. Even if you had full crews on the gun trucks, you couldn't dismount because you needed a minimum of two to stay on the vehicle (one to drive and one to man the weapon) and you would never dismount just one person – the buddy team is the lowest level the infantry plans to operate so that you can look out for and support each other.

Another big problem with the six vehicle configuration was the platoon leader, the commander of the unit, was not on a gun truck. The HMMWVs we had back then were not armored but the hard-top gun trucks provided some limited protection and a lot more firepower. The soft HMMWV was also known as a "command" vehicle and, with its multiple radio antennae, it was a high value target for any adversary who knew anything about our organizational structure. The guy in charge of this unit couldn't really lead it; he had to stay back and coordinate. "Leading from behind" was not (and is not) an effective plan.

I originally wanted to go to platoons of four gun trucks only, putting both the platoon leader and the platoon sergeant with a weapon and crew. When

I briefed the concept to the company leadership, all the senior NCOs said that the cargo HMMWV was essential to carry extra fuel, ammunition and missiles. I'm pretty sure that I had to balance both my communications and adaptability tendencies at this point but the bottom line is that I listened to them and changed the plan.

We knew that we wouldn't get any extra people to up the crew size to four people so we consolidated and became a company of four platoons with five vehicles each instead of five platoons with six vehicles each.

The battalion commander approved our concept and for the next two years, we trained on our new tasks and mode of operation. We started calling ourselves the battalion's "Motorized Rifle Company"[28] instead of the Anti-Armor Company because we wanted to put emphasis on the fact that we were infantrymen first and foremost. I was probably a pain in the ass for most of my peers but at every meeting or gathering, I insisted that Delta be seen as an equal to Alpha, Bravo and Charlie Companies.

So, there it was: our purpose had been redefined (by me) and approved by my boss. We went to his boss, the brigade commander, to recommend this new configuration and mission set become the standard for the brigade or even the division. He agreed to let us stay organized in the four platoon configuration but would not make the other two battalions change nor would he recommend it as the division standard.

This was great news for us because we continued to train and develop tactics and procedures to operate as a fighting unit. We worked hard that first six months because we knew that before the end of the summer of 1989, we would assume "mission" status and be on call to deploy anywhere in the world in eighteen hours or less.

We would have been battle tested in Panama when Operation Just Cause was executed in December of 1989 but that mission happened during the two weeks that our battalion was scheduled for "block leave;" the only two weeks between July of 1989 and February of 1990 that Just Cause could have happened and not include our battalion. To say we were disappointed would be an understatement but that is probably the case of all young men who don't know the true cost of war. Within nine months, we got our chance to go to war, which confirms the old adage: "Be careful what you wish for; it just might come true."

---

28. This was a play on the Soviet order of battle in that nearly all of their infantry were mounted on wheeled or tracked vehicles, even their airborne units. The wheeled units were known as Motorized.

Throughout the rest of 1990, we continued to train in this new fashion. We practiced dismounting our vehicles as often as possible and got ourselves ready for a training rotation to the Army's National Training Center (NTC) in the Mojave Desert. This would be a fight against armor forces in open desert terrain and I was extended in command so that I would take the company through this evaluation in the late summer of 1990.

The NTC rotation was canceled due to the disbanding of the Armor Brigade that our battalion was scheduled to support. The fall of the Berlin Wall a year before was starting to have its effect on the focus and thinking of the senior leadership. So, with no NTC rotation, my change of command date was set for late August of 1990.

On the 2nd of August 1990, Saddam Hussein invaded Kuwait and within a week, our company deployed to Saudi Arabia for Operation Desert Shield. As part of the 82nd Airborne's "Ready Brigade," we were the first combat troops on the ground: George H.W. Bush's famous "Line in the sand."

By the time we deployed, we had a new (and very nervous) battalion commander. He couldn't understand why "he" only had four Anti-armor platoons while the other two battalions had five. Five is more than four so certainly "he" had less than his peers.

I spent nearly every day trying to convince him that "he" had greater capability in our four platoons than the other battalions had with five. Our training and our mindset let us get to this point where we could take on any mission and succeed. We proved that during Desert Shield with every live-fire exercise[29] we executed and even during an external evaluation of all three Delta companies in the brigade.

The initiative that our men showed is evident in how we modified our .50 Cal vehicle mounts. At the time, we didn't have a way to stabilize and lock down the machine gun for more accurate fires. From a ground position on a tripod, stability (and accuracy) is gained using a traversing and elevating (T&E) mechanism which attaches to a cross bar on the tripod.

---

29 Known as an LFX for short, the live fire exercise is where soldiers practice with live ammunition against stationary and moving targets. It's as close to real combat as you can get without having the targets shoot back. I always tried to add more realism to these events but putting burning tires between the gunners and the target and having explosions and other weapons firing while the TOW gunners tracked their target.

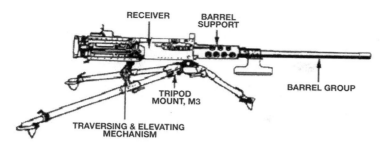

A key factor in an infantry assault of a defended position is something called the "support by fire" position where machine guns are massed to provide concentrated and deadly accurate fires at the point of penetration. This technique was perfected by Erwin Rommel in WWI and described in his book *Attacks*.

The organic machine guns in the rifle companies were the 7.62 mm M-60, an effective and generally reliable weapon but it lacked the range and punch needed to suppress an enemy position in open desert. That meant that Delta Company would have to use heavy machine guns to support the rifle companies, but we would have to dismount the weapon from the vehicle to gain the accuracy needed to support an assault without hitting our own men. Taking the initiative with our supply and maintenance staff at the battalion, my NCO's developed a system to keep the .50 Cal machine guns on the vehicles with the same accuracy as dismounting and putting them on a tripod.

With spare traversing bars welded to the ring mounts of the vehicle, we were able to attach the T&E mechanism to the weapon and get accurate fires out to 1500 meters and beyond from the vehicle. Without the vehicle mounts, we would have to "free gun" the weapon from the vehicle and there was no way we could provide safe and accurate fire. This also saved us a great amount of time in our battle drills. It takes time to dismount an M2. It weighs 127 pounds with the tripod and T&E and when you fire it, the barrel can get red hot so remounting it can be an adventure.

This was a clear example of soldiers taking the initiative to find a solution to a problem. They figured that there was a better way and they were going to find it. Our company kicked ass because they knew what they had to do and they knew why they were doing it.

As the months and weeks dragged on, we were happy that the Iraqi Army did not invade Saudi Arabia but we were not real happy to have to live in the desert away from family and home. We did make the most of that time to train and prepare ourselves for the combat that seemed imminent and it could have been a lot more intense than it turned out. Who knew that we would crush the Iraqi Army in just four days?

My greatest success as a company commander wasn't what we did during the war; it was that I was able to convince my boss not to make us change back to five platoons. We had been organized like this for nearly two years but he wanted us to go back to the old structure, not comfortable with the fact that he had fewer platoons than the other battalions.

There is adage that you "fight like you train." We were about to go to war with an tank and armored vehicle army that everyone called "battle-hardened" and he wanted us to fight in a way that we hadn't trained for in over two years. Clearly, his natural tendency for adaptability was rigid but we were able to get him to show some flexibility, even if he never really was happy about it.

When the war started and Desert Shield became Desert Storm, our brigade was attached to the French 6th Light Armor Division on the far western edge of the battlefield. For a month and a half, we conducted counter-reconnaissance and screening missions to prevent the Iraqi forces from knowing our full strength and disposition that far away from Kuwait and the sure knowledge that we were about to execute GEN Norman Schwarzkopf's famous "Left Hook."[30] These were exactly the missions that we had been training for since I took command.

The night before the ground campaign started (which for us was actually one day before the major push across the "berm" into southern Iraq and Kuwait), we were forward "screening" the rest of the brigade. Around midnight, I got a call from one of my platoons: contact. There was a vehicle and three dismounted figures moving across their front at about 2500 meters. This was the tactic we would expect to see from a reconnaissance unit – it's certainly how we would operate in unknown terrain. It turned out to be an Iraqi reconnaissance unit and, based on their uniforms and equipment that we later recovered, was probably from one of the elite Republican Guard divisions.

---

30 The term "left hook" is a boxing reference and it describes how Schwarzkopf and his war planners decided to liberate Kuwait by attacking through the desert in the west, or as you look at it on a map, from the left. The Iraqis were arrayed to defend against a direct assault on Kuwait and this "left hook" maneuver caught them off-guard and from an unexpected direction.

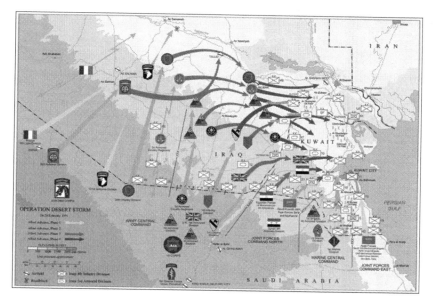

When I reported the contact higher, both the brigade and battalion commanders wanted us to engage with mortars. That would have been stupid and it was highly unlikely that we would have hit them; even if we did, we would have likely just warned them of our presence and sent them running. Their mission accomplished – they would have "found" us, reported the position and retreated.

I knew that we had the most accurate weapon system on the battlefield and this vehicle was in our crosshairs. More importantly Staff Sergeant Steve McLaughlin, the NCO in charge, and his crew knew what they needed to do and they knew how to do it. They were pressing me to authorize them to fire. I was ready to give that command but because of our tactical situation, I needed approval from the battalion, which needed approval from Brigade. It seemed to take forever but we finally got the approval to engage.

The Iraqi vehicle was now only 1500 meters out when the TOW missile was launched. I'll never forget the sound of the missile leaving the tube or of the flight motor kicking in. Little jets firing from the missile made a puffing/spitting sound as they fired to adjust the missile's course. Then, impact; an initial explosion as the missile made contact with the vehicle and then multiple secondary explosions as the rocket propelled grenades (RPGs) and shoulder-fired surface-to-air missiles (SAMs) cooked off in the back of the vehicle.

We sent that section forward: two vehicles and their crews moving mounted and dismounted to assess the damage and to look for the dismounted enemy soldiers or any survivors from the vehicle. They captured one of the three; the other two were probably captured the next day as thousands of Iraqi soldiers surrendered when the coalition advanced.

The rest is history as the Iraqi Army folded in four days. Our company moved forward with the rest of the brigade and the French to secure an airfield and then to link-up with the 101st, which had conducted deep helicopter movements (air assaults) to secure key terrain. Then we stepped back to let convoy after convoy of vehicles carrying fuel and ammunition go through to resupply the armor units farther to the east.

For me, the pride I felt wasn't so much for the speed at which we had won the war but how well my company had taken on its role to be the main effort in our battalion. In little more than two years, Delta Company went from being the problem company to the best at what we did. No organization could touch us for our ability to adapt, innovate and execute. This was all due to the men of my company taking on the responsibility to become masters of their trade and their tasks and understanding the purpose they served. Once they knew how to operate in this manner and why we needed to do it, I never had to tell anyone how to do something. It allowed me to command my company and not worry about control.

As they developed their skills and "know how" for fighting this way, and as I was able to lead by making sure they understood why we had to accomplish tasks and missions, I never had to go back to telling anyone how to do a task. Know how plus know why equaled "no how." Their readiness to innovate and work with purpose as their guide allowed me to be the fulcrum and maintain my natural tendency to command.

Self-Awareness

You Have a Tendency for Control If:

- You give very detailed instructions; all the time and to everyone
- You do tasks that you could (should?) delegate; you know the deal, if you want something done right…
- You constantly check up on people
- You show how "something" is done, not just tell what is to be done because after all, there is only one right way to do it
- You are a "details" person

You Have a Tendency for Command If:

- You tell people what needs to be accomplished; why not how
- You are comfortable delegating tasks
- You have people check in with you only when the task is complete or they have a problem only you can fix
- You don't worry (care?) about specifics in how things are done; there's a hundred different ways to do anything
- You are a "big picture" person

While this is one of the harder domains to change, it is one of the easiest to see in yourself and in others. It is also the one that we most easily fall into synch with our boss and that can be a good thing or it can be a very bad thing. The bottom line is that with regards to influence, the boss's style of leadership can have a huge impact on where we move our fulcrum.

I have a tendency towards command. I'm not all the way out on the edge of the lever but I'm closer to that than I am the center. That worked really well for me when I had subordinates that liked a lot of latitude and not a lot of direction. The kind of junior leader I worked best with was one that just wanted to know the mission (task and purpose) and what resources they had to accomplish it. This was my sweet spot too. Unfortunately, not everyone who worked for me could thrive in a command environment; they needed (craved) more direction than I was naturally inclined to give and when I didn't recognize that, they were not as good as they could have been and the team was not as good as it could have been – and all that was my fault.

The exclusive tendency in influence is marked by telling people what and how to do things while an inclusive tendency is to tell people what and why to do things. If you have a new team with little to no experience in the environment or with the tasks you find the organization operating in, you probably need to exercise more control. If you have a mature team with lots of experience in the environment or with the tasks you find the organization operating in, you probably need to exercise more command.

Something else to be aware of: do you have a tendency to accept influence in one fashion but exercise it in another? For example, is your tendency to be in the command state when you are given a mission and the control state when you are tasking a mission? This inconsistency is more common than you might think and unless it's really what the situation demands, it can be amended by a "Golden Rule" type of mindset to treat others as you want to be treated. We know all too well that type of leader whose motto seems to be: "do as I say, not as I do." Usually, this is a reference to people who hold others to a different standard of conduct but the standard or method of influence is subject to this motto as well. This inconsistency is a leadership version of cognitive dissonance: doing something that contradicts one or more of your beliefs or values.[31]

What kinds of instructions do you typically give? Do you trust people implicitly or do you check up on them? Are you more concerned with outcomes or process?

Most people will tell you that "trust must be earned..." but there is plenty of research to suggest that the easiest way to earn trust is to give it unconditionally.[32] If you are constantly telling people how to do things or if you are constantly checking up on them, their natural reaction is, "She doesn't trust me..." If your subordinates feel or think that they are not trusted, there is little chance they will take the initiative in anything or execute what they know needs to be done without first getting your approval (in writing or with a witness).

If you are concerned with the process of how things are done, or the details of how things are done, it is a likely indicator of your tendency to control. If we're talking about the operation of a nuclear power plant, or some other very technical function, attention to detail is a requirement and not necessarily a condition that would prevent you from a more command-like tendency but it is certainly an environment that can lend itself to more control.

Situational Awareness

See it in your team:

How experienced are the members of your team? Are your managers effective? How much initiative do your subordinates exercise? What kinds of questions do they ask?

One of the first assessments you will have to make once you become a s upervisor/manager, or if you move to a new lateral position or are promoted,

31 Kannan-Narasimhan, R.; Lawrence, B. S. (2012) "Behavioral Integrity: How Leader Referents and Trust Matter to Workplace Outcomes." *Journal of Business Ethics* Vol 111(2) November 2012

32. Dirks, D.T.; Ferrin, D. L. (2002) "Trust in Leadership: Meta-analytic Findings and Implications for Research and Practice." *Journal of Applied Psychology*, Vol 87(4), Aug 2002, 611-628

is to determine the maturity and skill level of your team. This is an exercise in group dynamics as well as individual ability. On the one extreme, your team will consist of veterans, skilled and experienced at what they do; you may in fact be the youngest person on the team. On the other extreme, your team is all rookies, with at best only the minimum required skills to get the job (which isn't the same as getting the job done) and you are as old if not older than your team members.

With skilled veterans, command is likely the best trait to exercise and with rookies, you will likely have to be more controlling. Failure to recognize this basic construct has been the downfall of many leaders. This is the obvious case for moving away from your natural tendency when it is out of balance with the situation. If you have a tendency to command but your people aren't ready for that kind of autonomy, they are likely to fail every mission because they don't know what to do or how to do it. Likewise, if you have a tendency to control and your team doesn't need that, you are likely to become marginalized by the team and they may very well slow down or quit.

The next assessment you need to make is how effective your team is. Again, this means looking at individual members of your team but also the team as a whole. It also requires an understanding of how static or dynamic your environment is. If your environment is static, an experienced team yesterday will be an experienced team tomorrow. If your environment is dynamic, yesterday's experience might be more of a problem than a help if your team members are complacent. That said, and I've talked about it already in these pages, the situation and environment are hardly ever static.

Changes in technology, changes in the competition and changes in the customer base will all have an impact on your situation and the type of influence you need to use. It might also require you to restructure your team or the roles of your subordinates within the team. While the term "talent management" is usually a reference to managing the careers of your people, in this case it means putting the right people into the right jobs based on their strengths and their weaknesses. If you have the ability to make these changes, you're likely to find it easier to maintain balance in the influence domain.

See It in Your Boss

A slight departure here from how we've been looking at the domains and a moment to talk about your boss.

As a subordinate or mid-level leader, your boss might just be the most important factor in your environment. She may expect you to exercise influence in the same way that she does and if that's different from your natural tendency, you'll probably have a problem dealing with her.

Does she check up on you often? What kinds of instructions does she give you? Does she care about process or the order in which things are done?

Answer these questions about your boss once you've asked them of yourself and look for the differences and similarities. If you are both the same, that's great if appropriate to the situation. If you are both exercising influence in a way that is out of balance with the situation, you've got to get her to move her fulcrum as well as moving your own. While it might be her expectation that you exercise influence in a way she is comfortable with, your success and the success of your team will ultimately rest with your ability to apply influence in a way that best fits the situation. Results matter more than process so you may need to work on your communication and focus tendencies when you go to convince your boss that you have the ability to deliver the best outcome using the amount and type of influence that is best.

Strategies for Being the Fulcrum with Influence

- Understand your purpose, the purpose of your team and its work
- Understand the desired outcome
- Understand how much time you have to achieve that outcome
- Understand your team (as individuals and collectively) and their skills, their maturity and their motivation
- Apply as much or as little control as needed depending on your team's abilities and the time allowed
- Communicate all that clearly to your team
- Ensure your team (collectively and as individuals) is ready to be more autonomous – never assume that they are willing and able to take on more responsibility

Understanding Purpose

In many ways, influence is the most important job of the leader. How we get people to do something they might otherwise not do; how we achieve a collective goal; how we see ourselves in the world. All these things happen with influence of some sort, sometimes directly and sometimes indirectly.

This makes purpose the driving force for influence: If you don't know your purpose, no amount or type of influence will allow you to achieve it.

Which way you move the fulcrum on influence, and how much or how little you direct, will be a function of your team and the task but every situation begins with "why." Your purpose must be understood and it must be believed. Otherwise, you are just exchanging a timecard for a paycheck. Simon Sinek explains this well in his book Start with Why and just as clearly but more succinctly is his TED Talk on the subject.

Understanding What You Want to Achieve

The second most important thing to understand is what success looks like. A vision of the outcome or end state is vitally important for any team doing any task but it is an essential element when the situation dictates more command and less control. Purpose and end state allow for the greatest amount of innovation and initiative within the team but they require that the team have the skills and maturity to work that way. Coupled with "why," the knowledge of where we want to go or what we want to be are your most powerful tools to exercise influence.

Know Your Time Horizon

An understanding of time is the next most critical factor in determining if and how far to move your fulcrum in influence. If you have a lot of time, you have a lot more options; you can use time and task to develop your team or to try new methods. If you have very little time, you will have fewer options on how to get things done and that might also drive you to being more controlling. Certainly, an individual or a team with little skill for a particular task and little time to accomplish an outcome will need more direction and more control. Even a person or a team with a lot of experience will sometimes need specific direction when time is of the essence. This is particularly important when a prioritization of resources or effort is needed – you as the leader must make that decision and ensure the team is on board.

These first three strategies mirror what you need to do for adaptability. The reason is because both are about accomplishing something: good decisions as a leader with adaptability and good outcomes as a team with influence. You may likely find yourself in a situation where you cannot be the fulcrum in one domain without being it in the other and the connections and overlap here should be helpful in that regard but don't confuse the two and what role they play in your role as leader. As you will see next, communications is closely linked to influence as well.

Get Your Message Out

How you communicate this is the next step and it reinforces the role of communications in leadership. Not only telling your people the why (purpose), what (end state), and if needed the how of a task but getting feedback so that you can adapt and change if need be. Here is where influence and communications work hand in hand. If you are not getting the feedback you need from your team, you might be too controlling or you might be too transmitting or perhaps you are both. Being the fulcrum for one can often help you with the other.

Readiness Level of Your Team

Finally, you must see where your team is in their desire to be more or less autonomous. If they don't want or are unable to take on more responsibility and ownership, you will need to be more controlling no matter if your tendency or desire is to be more commanding. In this case, you will have to use very direct guidance and look for members of the team who are looking for greater autonomy. It might be that you need to look for members of the team who just don't fit in or work well with the group. At that point, finding them some other place to use their talents might be best.

Ultimately, whatever your desire or tendency to influence as a leader, how you exercise it depends on the team you lead. On the face of it, commanding might be the preferred domain to operate in but that doesn't make it the best option when it's time to be the fulcrum.

SUMMARY

- Know your tendency
- Understand what the situation demands right now: direct or indirect influence?
- Know your purpose; make sure your team knows "why"
- Know the desired outcome
- Know how much time you have to achieve that outcome
- Know your team, as individuals and collectively, and assess their readiness for more autonomy
- Clearly communicate

CONCLUSIONS – BE THE FULCRUM

Congratulations, you've made it to the back of the book. Even if you started here to get an idea of what you are about to read, thanks for coming with me this far.

"Fulcrum-centric Leadership" and "Be the Fulcrum" are concepts that I've seen and experienced across nearly forty years as a student and practitioner of leadership. My observations and my actions, my leadership successes and my leadership failures all lead me to the firm belief that this is a complete but simple way to view what's important to know as a leader and how to find the best working solution when things are out of balance.

While the mechanics of a simple class one lever (a seesaw from our playground example) are that the fulcrum allows reduced effort to move a load, I don't want you to "Be the Effort" because sometimes balance requires us to give greater weight to the load or less effort to a particular tendency. And, we're not talking about just lifting or moving the load once. The point is that "Be the Fulcrum" is a way to remember that your goal is not just to lift or move the load (the situation) with your effort (usually your natural tendency) but to find and maintain balance as the situation changes and develops. It requires us to know ourselves and our tendencies, to know as much as we can about the situations where we lead and then to know when and how to "Be the Fulcrum."

I'm sure that some of you might be thinking that I have a bias or a preference for one tendency over another for each of our four domains. That's true, I do have a preference for one over the other – that's my natural tendency and that's the first point of my perspective. Except for where I thought it important to clarify my perspective, I believe that I've done a good job of keeping my tendencies to myself but because you are reading this book, I'm sure you are smart and observant and you may have seen something more than I intended. No matter, we all have a preference when it comes to these leadership domains. It might be a strong preference or it might be a mild preference but it's there and in order to be a better leader, we must know that tendency before we start trying to take charge of a situation.

If you come away from reading *Leadership in Balance* and get to this point thinking that "Mike is suggesting that this tendency is better than that tendency..." then I have failed to communicate the second key point of my perspective: The situation dictates what is positive or negative in leadership tendencies. Assessing the situation is as dynamic as it is critical; the environment, your team, your boss, your clients, your stakeholders, your competition are all changing all the time. Some changes are subtle and some changes are drastic but if you apply styles and techniques of leadership routinely because of their commonly assessed value, sooner or later you will fail as the situation gets and stays out of balance.

And if you have come this far in the book, I hope that you see the importance of applying what you know about your tendencies (the first point) with what you know about the situation (the second point) and that you become the fulcrum to restore balance to your leadership domains.

I know this works, not only because I've seen leaders do this and succeed but also because I've seen leaders fail who didn't do this, including me.

Looking back on my own leadership failures, it's clear to me now how most of them were the result of allowing my tendency in one or more of the domains to become that IFK. When I didn't recognize the situation for what it was or, worse, if I saw what was happening but I failed to be the fulcrum, I failed as a leader.

I can think of more than one occasion when I had a boss, usually with a tendency to transmit and not receive and I failed to recognize that I needed to transmit more or better to him. The situation often dictated that I communicate more clearly and in a way that my boss could understand – but I didn't. That's not to say that I am solidly on the receive end of the communications domain – just ask my wife – but in those situations where I failed, it was usually a failure to move more towards transmit. This goes back solidly to my point about quality versus quantity and treating the way other people process information like it's a foreign language. The same thing has happened when I didn't recognize the need to be the fulcrum with my subordinates and not transmitting what I needed to send when it was needed or in not picking up on the need to receive more or better information.

These situations with out-of-balance domains create leadership problems and challenges for us when we cannot see them or when we will not act to change them. We must be the fulcrum in these situations but often it doesn't happen because we are too slow to recognize the issue or unwilling to move away from our tendency, in either direction, when it is necessary.

For me this usually happened with the influence domain. My natural tendency is for command over control but the people who worked for me weren't always ready, willing and able to work with that. In many cases, the people working for me who were not ready to work in an environment where they could use their initiative and decide for themselves how to accomplish a task had worked previously for people who were very much in the control side of the influence domain. This is, or at least it used to be, very common in the Army. The terms "micro-management" and "zero-defects" describe this environment clearly because if in it, you are told how, not why, to do something and there is no room to learn and grow from the smallest mistake.

Having junior officers whose total leadership experience – or certainly their most recent – was working for someone whose tendency was strongly to control should have keyed me into the fact that I needed to exert some measure of control until they were ready to operate with more command. When I didn't do that, the team didn't perform as well as we could have and that probably had the effect of making my people even more tentative about working with less direct influence. In essence, my failure to be the fulcrum and shift away from my tendency for command made my team less effective.

In those situations, and only for as long as it took to achieve balance, I didn't acknowledge my tendency for command (I knew it but ignored its effect), I didn't properly assess the situation I was in and both those things prevented me from being the fulcrum. I'm thinking primarily of my time as a battalion commander here. By the time we deployed to Afghanistan in 2003, there were 1200 men (and some women) on my team. We accomplished all our missions and suffered no fatalities but we could have been better if I had been better balanced in how I worked in the influence domain of leadership.

Adaptability is my favorite of the four domains because it covers so much ground. The fact that encompasses decision making and judgment, key elements of what leaders get "paid" to do, makes it a very powerful domain.

When I first started to construct this perspective of leadership, I thought that I would call this domain "pride" because I was attempting to explain and describe how it is that some leaders will stick steadfastly to their decisions, even decisions that in time proved to be bad or even wrong. It seemed to me that pride was what kept them from admitting a mistake and doing something to correct it. I still believe that pride is a source of that stubbornness because when faced with overwhelming evidence that they zigged when they should have zagged, many leaders will not change from their original decision because of how that might make them look.

But as I started to work with the idea of adaptability and training soldiers to be more adaptive, it occurred to me that adaptability was a better and more encompassing domain for leadership. It covers the front-side and the back-side of decision making and judgment. It speaks to the idea of mindset and your ability to see failure as a learning opportunity.

It also gives us understanding when talking about leadership situations that being rigid or fixed in your decisions is not always a negative. The leader must have some idea of consequences and effects before a decision is made or before an action is taken. In doing so, the leader will anticipate short-term negative effects that are necessary for long-term positive effects. And in doing so, he or she can mitigate some of those short-term negatives.

So, success or failure as a leader depends greatly on adaptability because it can greatly affect the success of the team. Does the leader have the flexibility to make innovative choices? To adjust to conditions as they change? Does she have the strength to remain steadfast to an idea or an action when she knows it's the right or the best thing to do? Even when no one else sees it that way? These things defined some of my greatest success and my worst failings as a leader.

The same is true for the focus domain of leadership; my greatest failures as a leader happened when I didn't recognize that a situation demanded I shift to a more selfish effort in the focus domain. We value selfless service so highly in the Army that it is one of the seven core values. And in the long run or in "the greater scheme of things," it is absolutely the case that selfless is better than selfish.

But opportunity is often tied to ambition, desire and drive and what the individual wants to do for themselves. Afraid to do something in your personal interest and you are likely to stagnate in your career and fail to achieve your goals. The secret to this and finding balance is to understand how, when and why to do anything that puts your interests ahead of others.

There were times when I fell for the "be a team player" request from a boss or a peer only to have it cost me and my team – the people I was serving and leading – some opportunity. Let's be honest here and recognize that work can be a competitive endeavor as often, if not more often, as it is a collaborative endeavor. Resources and rewards in the real world are not unlimited and sometimes you have to fight for them or at the very least give a compelling argument as to why you and your team should get them. Remember that the "situation," all that stuff on the other side of the fulcrum, can include competitors and other elements of the environment that are not looking out for your best interest but their own.

I anticipate that this concept will be hard for some to accept and even harder for others to admit that they have acted at times in self-interest. "How can a guy who spent twenty-three years in the Army say that selfish could ever be a good thing?" That's easy; it's because I spent twenty-three years in the Army and the ten years since working with soldiers and civilians that I believe this. And again, I'm talking about situationally appropriate action. You as the leader still get to decide if you will shift your effort and be the fulcrum.

You can begin with self-awareness of your tendencies by taking the LFA. Once you know your natural tendency for each domain, you will be able to recognize your default style of leadership. You might also want to know what the natural tendencies of your team are, as individuals and collectively as a team. In this case we can provide you with a group license and the analysis to understand what that means to you as the leader.

I look forward to continuing the conversation at www.bethefulcrum.com where you will also find other valuable lessons and programs to help you on your leadership journey.

Glossary of Military Terms:

Assault: The last part of an offensive operation or attack to close with and destroy the enemy. It can also describe a type of insertion as in Airborne Assault (parachutes) or Air Assault (helicopters).

Battalion: A formation of troops generally 500 soldiers or more. A battalion will usually consist of three to five companies and is commanded by a Lieutenant Colonel (LTC/O-5 by rank or pay grade).

Brigade: A formation of troops generally 3000 to 5000 soldiers. A brigade will usually consist of three to six battalions and is commanded by a Colonel (COL/O-6 by rank or pay grade). In the current structure of the Army, the Brigade Combat Team (BCT) is the foundation for most combat operations and provides enabling capabilities to the battalions.

D3A: Decide, Detect, Deliver and Assess. This is the army's doctrinal methodology for targeting. It is a cyclic process.

Division: A formation of troops generally 10,000 to 20,000 soldiers. A division usually consists of three to six brigades and other smaller units and is commanded by a Major General (2-Stars) MG/O-8 by rank or pay grade).

F3EAD: Find, Fix, Finish, Exploit, Analyze and Disseminate. This is an emerging methodology to the targeting process. Like D3A, it is a cyclical process but uses language that operationalizes the process more clearly.

FOB: Forward Operating Base. A forward operating base (FOB) is any secured forward military position, commonly a military base, that is used to support tactical operations. A FOB may or may not contain an airfield, hospital, or other facilities.

NCO: Non-Commissioned Officer. NCO's are soldiers in the rank of Corporal (E-4) to Command Sergeant Major (E-9). NCO's are considered the "backbone" of the U.S. Army because it is a professional corps with the responsibility of training soldiers in their individual skills, maintaining standards and providing insight and guidance to the officers they serve with.

Officer: Officers hold commissions at their appointed rank and are the commanders of units. Officer ranks range from 2nd Lieutenant (2LT) to General (GEN).

Platoon: A formation of troops generally 25 to 50 soldiers. A platoon usually consists of three to five squads and is led/commanded by a 2nd or 1st Lieutenant (2LT or 1LT/O-1 or O2 by rank or pay grade).

Targeting: The process of finding and engaging targets of value with lethal or non-lethal means at a specific time and place for a specific outcome.

A more extensive list of terms can be found at: http://www.militaryterms.info/

References

Altucher, J. (2013), *Choose Yourself!: Be Happy, Make Millions, Live the Dream*, Lioncrest, ISBN: 978-1-61961-023-1

Branson, R. (2015), "Communication Is the Most Important Skill Any Leader Can Possess." (*Forbes Magazine*, JUL15): www.forbes.com/sites/carminegallo/2015/07/07/richard-branson-communication-is-the-most-important-skill-any-leader-can-possess/#7602dff74ff2

Goleman, D. (2015), *A Force for Good: The Dalai Lama's Vision for Our World*. Bantam Books, ISBN: 978-0-553-39489-4

Goleman, D., Boyatzis, R., McKee, A. (2013), *Primal Leadership: Unleashing the Power of Emotional Intelligence*, Harvard Business Review Press, ISBN: 978-1-4221-6803-5

Marquet, L. D.(2012), *Turn the Ship Around: A True Story of Turning Followers into Leaders*, Penguin, ISBN: 978-1-59184-640-6

Simmons, G. (2014), ME , Inc.: *Build an Army of One, Unleash Your Inner Rock God, Win in Life and Business*, Harper-Collins ISBN: 978-0-06-232261-6

Sinek, S. (2009), *Start with Why: How Great Leaders Inspire Everyone to Take Action*, Penguin, ISBN: 978-1-59184-644-4

Rand, A. (1961), *The Virtue of Selfishness*, Signet, ISBN: 978-0-451-16393-6

Rommel, E (1979), *Attacks*, Athena Press, ISBN: 0-9602736-0-3

ABOUT THE AUTHOR

Photo: Thomas Keever

Michael P Lerario

Mike Lerario was commissioned as an infantry officer in the United States Army in 1983 following graduation from the United States Military Academy at West Point, NY. He served twenty-three years on active duty, eleven of those years at Fort Bragg, NC, in the 82nd Airborne Division and at the Joint Special Operations Command (JSOC). He commanded two companies, the 82nd Airborne Division Long Range Surveillance Troop and D Company, 2nd Battalion, 325th Airborne infantry Regiment – the latter for thirty-one months including eight months in Saudi Arabia and Iraq for Operations Desert Shield/Desert Storm. Prior to returning to Fort Bragg in 2001, Mike served as the Operations Officer for Joint Task Force Full Accounting, the organization chartered to achieve the fullest possible accounting for our POW/MIAs from the Vietnam War. Mike commanded 2nd Battalion, 505th Parachute Infantry Regiment from June 2001 until July 2003, the last seven of those months in Afghanistan for Operation Enduring Freedom. He completed his military career in the Operations Directorate of JSOC where he returned again to Afghanistan and Iraq.

Upon his retirement from the Army in 2006, Mike went to work as a consultant and project manager for The Wexford Group International, providing specialized consulting services in defense related subjects to the Department of Defense and to NATO. In 2013 he deployed to Afghanistan as an operational advisor to the NATO Special Operations Component Command Afghanistan (NSOCC-A) and again in 2014 as Senior Command Advisor to the Commander, ISAF Joint Command.

In 2014 he founded Crispian Consulting, Inc. and serves as president and principal consultant. Crispian Consulting provides military and defense subject matter experts to a wide range of clients including technology companies, professional sports teams and government agencies. Crispian also provides coaching, training and assessments in leadership development for individuals and organizations.

In addition to his work with Crispian Consulting, Mike is a Director for Leadership Development with All American Leadership, LLC; he serves on the Community Advisory Board for the *Fayetteville* (North Carolina) *Observer* editorial board; he works as an adjunct researcher for the RAND Corporation and is also an adjunct faculty member at Fayetteville State University in the School of Business and Economics.

Mike holds a Bachelor of Science in Engineering and a Master of Arts in Leadership Development, both degrees from the United States Military Academy at West Point, NY.

He and his wife, Martha, have been married for thirty-two years and have two sons and two grandchildren.

Made in the USA
San Bernardino, CA
26 October 2016